MW01167668

WHAT KIDS NEED TO KNOW ABOUT BLACK HISTORY

DISCOVER 40 INSPIRING BLACK HEROES,
LEADERS & INVENTORS WHO SHAPED OUR
WORLD - FROM THE 1300'S TO TODAY!

HILLCREST HISTORY

PUBLISHED BY HILLCREST HISTORY

CONTENTS

INTRODUCTION

"Those who have no record of what their forebears have accomplished lose the inspiration which comes from the teaching of biography and history. When you control a man's thinking, you do not have to worry about his actions. The mere imparting of information is not education."

Carter G. Woodson

People of African heritage have made a significant contribution and have helped shape Western history for centuries, but these roles have often been overlooked or distorted in the American and European consciousness. Black History Month, however, as an annual celebration of this important contribution, helps to redress the balance.

It was conceived by the "Father of Black History," Carter G. Woodson. Born in Virginia in 1875, Carter's parents had both been enslaved. He grew up in poverty with limited opportunities, but by working in a coal mine, he managed to save enough money to pursue an education at one of the few high schools for Black children, starting at the age of twenty.

He had a deep passion for learning. After teaching school-children, he studied for a bachelor's degree at Berea College in Kentucky, a master's degree at the University of Chicago, and finally, he earned a PhD at Harvard in 1912, becoming the second African-American to achieve such a doctorate.

He co-founded the Association for the Study of African American Life and History, an organization dedicated to studying Black heritage. In 1926, he conceived the idea of celebrating and promoting his subject during a special week in February each year. He chose February since it was the birth month of former President Abraham Lincoln, who opposed slavery during the American Civil War, and the birth month of the formerly enslaved Frederick Douglass, who became a statesman, writer, and abolitionist. He founded the American Equal Rights Association and famously said, *"The white man's happiness cannot be purchased by the Black man's misery."*

Fifty years later, Black History Week was relaunched as Black History Month by former President Gerald Ford, carrying forward with the same values to *"honor the too-often neglected accomplishments of Black Americans in every area of endeavor throughout our history" and as* a timely reform as Black history had all too often focused on slavery and oppression, which are vital aspects, but there is so much more to be studied, analyzed and celebrated, in every era.

Black History Month is a mainstay in schools, colleges, and the wider community. It involves museums, civic institutions, and libraries hosting exhibitions, events, and workshops while theatres and cinemas present programs that mark Black History Month's annual chosen theme. These themes have ranged from "Health and Wellness" to "Black Resistance" and "Ours to Tell" to "The Black Family."

"Black History Stories" relates the lives and experiences of forty Black people who have made their mark on our history. We have included famous, well-known leaders and activists, modern-day celebrities, and people you might not have heard of, but each one has a place in the story of how our world and society have evolved over the ages.

We hope you enjoy reading about these remarkable and inspirational people.

Let's go back to

THE
1300'S -
1800'S

1

MANSA MUSA - THE RICHEST MAN WHO EVER LIVED

In 1312, Mansa Abu-Bakr II, the ninth ruler of Mali, prepared a fleet of more than 2000 boats with enough gold, food, and water to last for several years and, with thousands of men, women, and slaves, set sail on a great expedition to find what lay beyond the Atlantic Ocean. He left his younger brother, Musa, to rule his kingdom in his absence, and he—and his fleet—were never to return, though there are legends that he did manage to reach the Americas.

Mansa Musa (in Mandinka, "Mansa" means sultan or emperor) became the new sovereign of Mali's immense empire; under his rulership, these lands expanded even further. From the Atlantic coast, his territories extended across Africa. They included parts of modern-day Senegal, Mauritania, Burkina Faso, Niger, The Gambia, Guinea-Bissau, Guinea, and the Côte d'Ivoire—a land so vast it would take more than a year to travel from one end to the other, around 3,000 km. During Mansa Musa's reign, many communities, hoping for a better quality of life, were pleased when their lands became a part of the great Mali Empire.

These lands provided Mansa Musa with the most fabulous wealth imaginable. In the north, his territories were rich in salt, while in the south, there were gold and copper mines and vast quantities of elephant ivory—among the most highly prized resources in the world. It is almost impossible to calculate exactly how rich he was; his treasure and land holdings were deemed "indescribable."

Despite his colossal wealth, the emperor was a devout and pious man, devoted to his Muslim faith, and in 1324, he decided to make a hajj to Mecca. This would be a pilgrimage like no other. His procession of 60,000 men— his entire court of soldiers, griots, officials, traders, and 12,000 slaves were dressed in sumptuous costumes of Persian silk and gold brocade. A hundred camels, carrying large bags filled with gold, were followed by thousands of animals, goats and sheep, that would feed his entourage. Mansa Musa himself rode on horseback behind 500 enslaved people, each carrying a golden scepter.

From his capital city of Niani, on the left bank of the Sankarani River, the glittering procession made their way to Walatah in Mauritania and then to Touat in central Algeria before arriving in Cairo, with a great deal of ceremony.

The people of Egypt had never seen anything like it. But the young king was not just a glorious spectacle of wealth. He was incredibly generous and handed out so many gifts of gold during his stay that the price of gold in North Africa nosedived and did not recover for twelve years. The Sultan of Cairo, Al-Malik Al-Nasir, was initially concerned about the intentions of his visitor to his country, but he couldn't help but respect Mansa Musa's respectfulness and devotion to his faith.

The *jelis*, Malian griots, who were employed to compose songs to tell of the emperor's adventures, however, were not quite as supportive. It is said that they were reluctant to praise his extravagance and wasteful generosity toward those outside his empire.

Stories of the emperor and his lavish spending even reached Europe, and a Catalan map drawn in 1375 includes the Kingdom of Mali with an illustration of a king sitting on a golden throne with a piece of gold in one hand and a golden staff in the other on the area marked "Timbuktu."

Returning from Mecca, the procession passed through Cairo again. Whether it was because he had spent so lavishly during his trip or in an attempt to help stabilize the dip in the economy he had caused during his last stay, he bought a large quantity of gold from Egyptian lenders at an exorbitant interest rate.

As they headed across Africa, one of Mansa Musa's generals captured the city of Gao, the capital of the Songhai Province, to the delight of the emperor, and rather than return directly to Niani, the procession was diverted there so he could accept the surrender of the king in person.

During this Hajj, Islamic scholars, some direct descendants of the Prophet Muhammad, and Abu Haq Es Saheli, the poet and architect from Grenada, were persuaded to return to Mali with Mansa Musa's procession. In Gao, a mosque was built using burnt bricks, marking the first time such materials were being used for building in Africa. Usually, structures in Africa were fabricated from beaten earth and wooden supports.

When he returned to the capital, Mansa Musa looked toward improving his great kingdom. He commissioned Abu Es Haq se Saheli to construct the Djinguereber mosque at Timbuktu and paid him 200 kg of gold for his efforts. He also built a palace with fortifications that stretched from Niani to Timbuktu to provide protection against the marauding Tuareg tribes of the southern Sahara. He also had public buildings, such as schools and libraries, for his people and encouraged the scholars he had brought to his lands to produce literature and art.

He divided his expansive empire into provinces, and for each, he appointed a *farba*—a governor he knew and trusted—to oversee the welfare of his subjects, taxes on trade, and production in the cold and copper mines, which created even greater wealth for the empire.

Little is known about the wealthiest man to have lived other than a few contemporary accounts, such as that of Arab historian Al-Makrizi, who met Mansa Musa in Cairo and described him as having "a pleasant face and a good figure...," but he couldn't help ending his observations with a mention of the emperor's riches; "his gifts amazed the eye with their beauty and splendor."

When he died, probably in 1332, Mansa Musa's sons inherited his lands, but the empire soon began to crumble without his strong and intelligent leadership. The fabulous wealth was no longer confined to his Keita dynasty, and many of the mines that had provided the gold and copper for the emperor would guild other kings, queens, and companies.

But Mansa Musa left a great legacy. He is not just remembered as the glittering sun king who took his great court across the desert, loaded with gleaming, unimaginable riches, but as the founder of modern education in West Africa. Not only did he bring intellectuals and scholars back from his hajj, but he also sent his own people to Fez in Morocco to study Koranic theology and law. When they returned, they became teachers in schools or at the Sankoré University that he established in Timbuktu. This would become an internationally renowned center of Islamic culture and religious learning, and Timbuktu became the holiest city in Western Africa.

NYATSIMBA MUTOTA - A COUNTRY BUILT ON SALT

The Kingdom of Mutapa (also known as Mwenemutapa) was an African kingdom in Zimbabwe that expanded to the east as far as what is now Mozambique.

According to stories passed down in the Shona oral tradition, it was founded at the beginning of the 15th century by a young warrior prince called Nyatsimba Mutota. His father, King Nyanhewe Matope of Zimbabwe, was old and gravely ill when he sent his son to leave his lands in search of salt to help his people, who were starving. Salt has been a crucial resource in Africa since ancient times. It was used as a seasoning and to preserve food, which was so valuable to some cultures that it was even used as a form of currency.

The prince and his followers headed north, and he came across a tribe of elephant hunters who told him that he would find salt at the river. The quest continued until, eventually, they reached a delta of the Zambezi, where saltwater from the Indian Ocean had penetrated the marshes around the river banks.

Prince Mutota laid claim to this valley, then built a settlement at Mount Fura, and from there, the Kingdom of Mutapa was founded.

As well as salt, this region had plenty of wild game and gold deposits ready to be mined. The Bantu-speaking people who already inhabited the land integrated well with the Zimbabwean newcomers, and a thriving society quickly began to develop. The new kingdom was rich in natural resources, and its people were content to build gold mines, smelt iron, and raise cattle. Before long, a lucrative commercial trade network was formed, and through these enterprises, good relations with other African cultures were fostered.

Although no known contemporary accounts describe the capital city of Zvongombe, built by King Mutota, Portuguese explorers who visited in the years that followed wrote about this city. They described it as so large that it took an hour to walk around and how it was enclosed by a great wooden barrier fence. Within this stockade, there were three immense buildings. The first was the main palace where the king held court; the second was for his wives and advisors, which housed around 3,000 people, and the third was for the attendants and pages that served the king and his bodyguards. These young men were selected from his kingdom for their strength and vitality and would later be trained as soldiers of Mutapa.

The people of Mutapa believed in the deity Mwari as their supreme being, the giver of rain, and the controller of fertility. Both male and female, Mwari was the god of darkness and light, the skies and the earth, and the author of all things. They saw Mwari as a kind and loving god. King Mutota ruled over his kingdom in the spirit of his faith. He was wise, benevolent, and clever. He controlled trade over his large kingdom by introducing state-sponsored markets, called *feiras,* along the river, so at Luanze, Dambarare, and Masappa, traders could buy and sell their wares. Archeological excavations have discovered iron tools, blue and white Chinese porcelain, and glass beads that were fashioned in India, which found their way to market in Mutapa.

After his death, the king's son, Mwened Matope, inherited the kingdom and fought several tribes in the surrounding areas to expand Mutapa and, at its greatest, the countries now known as Angola, Zambia, Zimbabwe, and part of Mozambique; the Zambezi river valley to the Indian Ocean were all a part of the new empire. King Matope's regal costume included symbols of his majesty, his land, animal horns, spears, and representations of granaries, as well as a ceremonial belt adorned with a beautifully decorated farming implement, similar to a hoe, with an ivory handle.

However, the great, peaceful kingdom of Mutapa was not destined to last. By the middle of the century, King Mutota's descendants proved to be weak leaders, and the empire's provinces began to break away. Their governors became greedy for more power, and eventually, European invaders destroyed all that was left of their legacy.

3

ALESSANDRO DE' MEDICI - THE BLACK DUKE

In the 16th century, Florence was the European center of finance, learning, and, especially, painting and sculpture. It was ruled by the bourgeois Medici family, one of the most powerful in European history who are remembered for their generous patronage of the arts, their immense wealth, and their ruthless scheming. This was an ambitious family that provided Renaissance popes, royal queens, great leaders, and vicious murderers, and in 1532, one of these Medicis became the first Black European head of state.

Alessandro de' Medici was born in 1510, in Florence. His mother was an African servant (or possibly an enslaved person), thought to be called Simunetta, and his father was said to be Lorenzo de Piero de' Medici, although it is more likely to have been Guilio de' Medici who became Pope Clement VII.

Alessandro, as an illegitimate son, had a remarkable rise to power; his cousin, Ippolito (also illegitimate), had been the family heir until Pope Clement fell ill and feared his family might lose their grip as head of the Catholic church, so he made Ippolito a cardinal with a view to him becoming a future pope. This left Alessandro as the potential Medici ruler of Florence but only after the political situation had improved; the city was unsettled under the rule of another family, and the Medicis had to bide their time preparing to take back control. Ippolito, however, was furious to be shackled to the church and never forgave the Pope or his cousin, Alessandro. It has often been said that the two men had hated each other since they were boys. Ippolito never stopped scheming against Alessandro for revenge and hoping to seize Florence for himself.

In May 1527, a revolution broke out in Florence, and the Medici family, including Alessandro, fled. Pope Clement managed to persuade the Holy Roman Emperor, Charles V, to send his army to restore order to the city. As part of these negotiations, a marriage was arranged between Margaret, the emperor's young daughter, and Alessandro, whom he nominated as Duke of Florence.

Alessandro assumed this title on 1 May 1532 at the age of nineteen. He was a fair ruler, and because of his efforts to help the poor and helpless, he became well respected by his people. He was cultured, intelligent, and a close friend of Giorgio Vasari, the painter, architect, and biographer of the great names of Renaissance art. Because of his African heritage, he was often known as "Il Moro" ("the Moor").

He had a lot of enemies, however. Some believed he did not have a rightful claim to his title because of his illegitimacy, which always seemed to be a greater obstacle than his skin color and ancestry. After Pope Clement died in 1534, Ippolito did his best to have his cousin discredited, but with Charles V supporting Alessandro, there was little he could do. He died of a fever the following year, and many believed that Alessandro had arranged for him to be poisoned.

Other Florentine families, living in exile, spread rumors about his incompetent, overly harsh leadership and suggested he was corrupt and, since he kept a mistress (with whom he had had three children) and had enjoyed affairs with several women, immoral.

He had a great friend, Lorenzino de' Medici, another cousin who was a writer and dramatist. The two men were so close; they were seen riding the same horse together in Florence, but unknown to Alessandro, the treacherous Lorenzino was planning to kill him.

On the evening of the 5 January 1537, Lorenzino lured his cousin to his lodgings, claiming a beautiful widow wanted to meet him there. While he was waiting, Alessandro fell asleep. During the night, Lorenzino arrived with a hired assassin named Scoronconcolo, and they attacked the sleeping duke. Alessandro did his best to fight them, even biting off a part of his cousin's finger, but after a violent struggle, he was stabbed to death.

Alessandro's remains were buried in his father's tomb in the Basilica of San Lorenzo in Florence. Lorenzino, from then on known as "Lorenzaccio"—or "bad Lorenzo"—fled from Florence and, in Venice, wrote his "Apology," explaining that he had been compelled to murder Alessandro to free Florence from his tyrannical rule. He, too, was murdered in 1548 in revenge for the murder of the Duke of Florence.

Alessandro, as the Duke of Florence, might have been a great leader if he had lived. However, in the cut-throat, Machiavellian world of the Medici, he never had the chance. Interestingly, a remarkable leader emerged within his household. His widow, who was just fifteen years old when he died, would become the Governor of Holland—a very unusual position of great responsibility and status for a woman in Renaissance Europe.

4

GASPAR YANGA - BREAKING THE CHAINS

Nyanga, a royal prince of Gabon, was captured and sold into slavery in the middle of the 16th century and then shipped to Mexico as part of the Iberian Trans-Atlantic slave trade, assuming the most appalling conditions.

Upon arriving in Mexico, he was given the name Gaspar Yanga and put to work in the Veracruz sugar plantation. The work was hard, and the enslaved workers were subjected to cruel and brutal treatment with severe punishments for anyone breaking the rules or trying to escape.

However, in 1570, Yanga, as he was known, had had enough. He and a group of companions broke free from the plantation. They fled to the mountains near Córdoba, where they established a peaceful, isolated shelter for formerly enslaved people, including Africans who had been shipped to Mexico, as well as indigenous people captured by the Spanish for labor.

Yanga, as a leader, oversaw the building of the settlement or *"pelanque"* and the farming of the surrounding land to support his people. They are thought to have grown sweet potatoes, beans, sugar cane, chillis, squash, corn, and tobacco. There, they lived for almost forty years, relatively untroubled by the Spanish overlords who owned the plantations, and by 1609, around 500 Black men were living in this mountain community.

The Spanish overlords, however, began to lose patience with Yanga's people, stealing from their estates and plantations, looting goods being transported on the main road from Veracruz to Mexico City, and "kidnapping" indigenous women. There had been rumors for years that the Black people that they had enslaved were preparing a large-scale revolt that would culminate in the murder of the Europeans and the crowning of one of their own people as king. To try and put an end to any possible plans, the Spanish increased the severity of punishments for any plantation workers trying to escape: brutal whippings and fastening weights to the feet of those caught absconding. They also decided to show that they would not tolerate any disobedience by putting an end to Yanga's *palenque* in the mountains.

In 1609, armed Spanish soldiers advanced to the mountains, intending to burn down the settlement, but Yanga's warriors fought against them and were defeated. Just as the Spanish had heard rumors of an uprising, Yanga's people had heard that Black people who had rebelled against the enslavers were being dismembered and nailed to pieces along the main roads to serve as an example to the rebels. They believed they would be fighting for their lives.

The Spanish militia made several more attacks, but the *Yanguicos*—as they became known—doggedly defended their land and their freedom, and as the Europeans were beginning to realize that it was hopeless trying to continue, Yanga saw this as his opportunity and offered peace terms with eleven conditions; first and foremost was the guaranteed freedom of all his people at the *palenque* and that his settlement would be recognized as a legal township, under his responsibility, and home for his and his people's descendants. In return, Yanga agreed to acknowledge the Spanish sovereignty in Mexico and fight on behalf of the Spanish if they were attacked.

The negotiations took time, but in 1618, the town of San Lorenzo de Los Negros was officially recognized by Spanish authorities as a free black settlement on the condition that Catholic Franciscan priests should be allowed to attend to their spiritual needs and that they did not actively encourage other laborers on the plantation to leave and join them. In later years, the Spanish tried to break this agreement several times, but the town remained free, and over time, it came to be called Yanga.

Yanga was not the only enslaved African to rebel against the abhorrent slavery in 16th-century South America, but he was certainly among the most successful. His name has been a symbol of freedom for Black and African

Mexicans. In 1871, he was named a "national hero of Mexico." In Yanga's town, he is represented by a statue of a strong, powerfully built Black man, holding a machete as if ready to cut through the chains of slavery.

5

YASUKE - BLACK SAMURAI

 "For a Samurai to be brave, he must have a bit of black blood."

- An old Japanese proverb

The Samurai were the great warriors of Japan, honored since the 8th century for their bravery and selflessness. In the 16th century, the first foreign-born Samurai would be the legendary Yasuke.

THE STORY of Yasuke's life before he came to Japan is quite a mystery. It is most likely that he came from Mozambique since they were the first Africans to reach that part of Asia as sailors or enslaved people aboard Portuguese ships, but from the descriptions of his height and color, he could have been a Dinka from South Sudan or perhaps Ethiopian, particularly since the name Yasuke is known to have been used in that country at the time.

HE ARRIVED in Japan in 1579 with Alessandro Valignano, a Jesuit missionary, who employed him as his valet and bodyguard. When the Japanese people saw Yasuke, they were astonished at his appearance; he was extremely tall and well built, with very dark skin, and since representations of Buddha were often black, they wondered if this handsome Black giant might be some kind of god.

AS THEY REACHED the Catholic mission in Kyoto (then the capital of Japan), word had spread about him, and crowds amassed, hoping for a glimpse of this remarkable stranger. Amid the commotion, people were crushed to death, and buildings collapsed with the weight of spectators desperate to see.

AS YASUKE RODE through the city on his horse, one of the most powerful *daimyo* warlords in Japan, Oda Nobunaga, was at his temple of Honnō-Ji and, when he heard the commotion, commanded that Yasuke should be brought before him.

WHEN THE TWO MEN MET, Nobunaga was pleased to be able to speak with his visitor. In the short time Yasuke had been in Japan, he had learned the Japanese language and understood and respected many of the country's traditions. But all the while, Nobunaga was fascinated by his visitor's skin. Eventually, he asked Yasuke to strip to the waist and studied him closely. He still couldn't quite believe such black skin could be real and asked for Yasuke to be scrubbed, thinking he might have stained himself with ink or charcoal. Once he realized it would not wash away, he ordered a great feast to be prepared in Yasuke's honor.

NOBUNAGA ALSO GAVE his new friend gifts and money, then arranged for him to leave Alessandro Valignano's service to become his own weapon bearer, culturally a position of great honor, privilege, and responsibility.

YASUKE QUICKLY PROVED HIS WORTH; he was trustworthy and diligent, and within a year, he was rewarded with a home in Azuchi Castle in the northeastern province of Kyoto, a regular salary, and a katana sword, the symbol of the Samurai.

IT WAS NOT long before Yasuke was called to fight as a Samurai. He and Nobunaga joined other forces against the Takeda warriors for territory in the Mount Fuji region, and then, in June 1582, Nobunaga's large army prepared for war against another enemy, the Mori.

. . .

THIS WAS to be Nobunaga's last battle. He had arrived with his advance party, including Yasuke, but they were quickly overwhelmed. Nobunaga's temple at Honnō-Ji was in flames, and many of his men had been slain. To preserve his honor, in keeping with the Samurai code, Nobunaga performed *seppuku*, ritual suicide, and his son, Nobutanda, was appointed the head of the Oda warriors.

BY THEN, however, losses were so great that Nobutanda, like his father, also performed *seppuku* that very same day in the face of defeat. Yasuke was captured and made to stand before the enemy. Because he had handed over his katana sword in the Western tradition, the victorious general refused to pass judgment on him since he was clearly not Japanese and commanded that he should be returned to Alessandro Valignano at the Jesuit missionary outpost, just where he had started; his short career as a Samurai was over.

NOTHING IS KNOWN of Yasuke afterward. His final years remain as much a mystery as his youth. His story has fascinated researchers and historians for centuries, and his life has been the subject of many books, films, and animations.

6

NZINGA MBANDE - WARRIOR QUEEN

When Nzinga Mbande was born in 1583. Her birth had been difficult; her umbilical cord had been wrapped around her neck. Her father was the King of Ndongo, and her mother was his favorite concubine. According to the country's superstitions, royal children who survived traumatic births were believed to possess special spiritual gifts and were born with great power. Nzinga certainly fulfilled these prophecies.

When Portuguese colonialists arrived in Ndongo in 1575, they established a trading post in Luanda. By the 1580s, they had burned down several villages and seized large areas of land upon which they had built forts to defend their gains. They had also enslaved thousands of people— possibly more than 50,000.

Nzinga became a great favorite of her father's, and he had delighted in giving her a thorough education; she was trained as a warrior, she could skilfully handle the Ndongo traditional battle axe, he had taught her diplomatic and governance skills, and she had learned to read and write Portuguese from visiting missionaries.

Nzinga's father died in 1617, and her brother, Mbandi, became king. He began his reign with a brutal campaign to remove anyone who might threaten his throne and killed several members of his family, including Nzinga's young son. She and her two sisters were spared, but only after they had been forcibly sterilized. Then, he had them banished to the Kingdom of Matamba.

Mbandi then turned his attention to his kingdom and the possibility of retaking some of the territory that had been lost to the Portuguese. In 1621, he reached out to Nzinga and asked her to negotiate with them since she spoke their language and, as a member of the royal family, should command respect.

She arrived in Luanda in her magnificent traditional dress (rather than European clothes that were customarily worn during such negotiations) and a large retinue, whom the Portuguese governor was expected to accommodate at some expense.

However, when she met with the Portuguese officials, they did not provide her with a chair—a deliberate gesture to let her know that they saw her as a subordinate. Nzinga, however, directed one of her attendants to kneel on all fours, and she sat upon them as though they were a chair. She then skilfully managed the negotiations to secure peace for the people of Ndongo with all the diplomatic tact she had learned as a girl.

The Portuguese could not fail to be impressed by Nzinga's eloquence and regal demeanor (completely different from that of her brother, the king). Consequently, they agreed to end hostilities, remove their Ndongo forts, and, in return, she would allow their slave traders into her country while the Portuguese hostages held in Ndongo would be returned. To prove her commitment, Nzinga agreed to be publicly baptized and then returned to Kabasa with her treaty.

Peace in Ndonga did not last. The fierce Imbangala people had made a series of attacks to expand their kingdom and, having taken Kasaba, forced the royal family into exile. The Portuguese governor offered to help but on the condition that the king should be baptized, but Mbandi could not bring himself to move so far from the traditions of his country and fell into a deep depression.

Nzinga took control. In 1624, Mbandi died unexpectedly after naming her his successor. She gave him an opulent funeral and then arranged for his young son to be killed in front of her, probably an act of revenge for the death of her own son and to remove a potential threat to her leadership.

It was a difficult time for Ndonga. The people were uneasy with Nzinga's willingness to negotiate with the Portuguese, but when the governor began to break some of the terms they had agreed in their treaty, they quickly realized that she was by no means a weak leader, as she stood firm against them.

On 15 March 1626, the Portuguese declared war on Nzinga. Nzinga's forces were initially defeated, and she sent an envoy with an offer of peace terms, but he was executed soon after he arrived in Luanda. The enemy insisted she should abdicate from her throne in favor of a nobleman they had befriended and would govern the country to their advantage.

Nzinga, after some soul searching, began to rebuild her armies and tried to fight against the Portuguese, but she had little success. By the end of 1628, all seemed hopeless, and she was expelled from Ndonga, along with what was left of her army.

A powerful Imbangala warlord, Kasanje, approached Nzinga with the offer of an alliance and marriage, which introduced her to another new culture. With this Imbangala support, she conquered the Kingdom of Matamba and, from there, continued to battle against the European oppressors.

As her military strength grew, she began to supply enslaved people to Dutch traders, who had arrived in West Africa hoping to push the Portuguese aside, and in 1641, they seized the Luanda trading post. Nzinga proposed an Afro-Dutch alliance against the Portuguese. With the wealth she accumulated from the sale of enslaved people and the military supplies she bought from the Dutch, she quickly reversed her fortunes and became a very powerful ruler with a great army.

In 1644, she defeated the Portuguese at the Battle of Ngoleme, but she was defeated at the Battle of Kavanga.

Two years later, her sister, Funji, was captured and drowned in the Kwanza River as a punishment for spying. Nzinga's Dutch allies sent reinforcements; however, her army continued to fight. In 1648, the Portuguese king sent a new governor who besieged Luanda and, unbeknown to Nzinga, negotiated with the Dutch, who agreed to leave.

In 1651, after being at war for almost twenty-five years, Nzinga and the Portuguese finally settled their differences. She spent her later years rebuilding her kingdom, resettling formerly enslaved people as workers on her war-ravaged lands, and she transformed Matamba into an important trading center. She believed in the importance of education and moved away from some of Ndango's old customs and beliefs.

Throughout the long years of conflict, Nzinga had dressed as a man and insisted her female attendants should do the same (while her sixty male concubines were made to wear traditional feminine dress). However, no longer at war, she began to dress as a woman again.

Nzinga died on 17 December 1663. Since then, her life has been well documented in Africa and Europe. She is remembered as a strong, intelligent ruler as capable as a diplomat as she was as a warrior and devoted to her people. Her fight for independence and dogged determination not to give in has long been an inspiration to the people of Angola and Africa.

7

ABRAM PETROVICH GANNIBAL - CHANGING FORTUNES

Like so many enslaved people in history, little is known of Abram Petrovich Gannibal's early life. He is thought to have been born around 1697 in East Africa, perhaps in Ethiopia or Sudan, into a wealthy and powerful Muslim family. His given name, "Abram," may have originally been Ibrahim.

Abram was captured by Turks from the Ottoman Empire as they ransacked his father's lands. He was taken to Constantinople, a horrendous journey during which his sister was drowned at sea. Soon after his arrival, he was bought by Sultan Ahmed III and made to work in his royal court. Abram was a very intelligent boy with respectful manners that brought him to the attention of the Russian emissary who was visiting the sultan on behalf of Peter the Great.

The tsar had asked for a few "clever" Black enslaved boys to serve at his court, thinking they would bring a new and exotic flavor to his palace. Abram, with two other boys, was selected for him. During the long period of traveling to the Russian capital, Abram was quick to learn Russian words and phrases, and when he was finally presented to Peter the Great, the tsar took a particular interest in the young boy.

Abram accompanied the tsar on his military campaigns, often as his valet, and they developed a close relationship. In 1705, Abram was baptized at St. Paraskeva Church in Vilnius with Peter the Great as his godfather. From then on, he used the date of his baptism as his birthday since he did not know his actual date of birth.

By 1717, Abram spoke several languages, and believing he would have a great future in the military, the tsar sent him to Paris to study warfare, science, mathematics, and art. He was an excellent student with a particular gift for engineering, and to gain practical experience, he joined the French army the following year. While he served, fighting against the Spanish in the War of the Quadruple Alliance, he also continued to develop his understanding of military technology until, in 1722, he suffered a head injury.

Once he had recovered, Abram threw himself into his studies. He developed a deep admiration and respect for the Carthaginian General Hannibal, one of the greatest military leaders in history, and began to call himself "Gannibal" as a tribute. Abram was in Paris during the Enlightenment, an intellectual and philosophical movement that completely reshaped how people understood issues, such as liberty, equality, and individual rights. He met and befriended some of its main thinkers, including Voltaire, who called him the "dark star of the Enlightenment."

He left Paris and returned to Russia, ready to share his knowledge and theories with the Russian court. But in 1725, his great friend and champion, Peter the Great, died, leaving his wife, Catherine I Tsarina, supported by Prince Menshikov, who had always resented Abram (as a non-Russian) and had him exiled to Siberia.

Abram spent several years in the Russian Far East developing his construction and engineering theories, oversaw the building of a fortress, and even made a study of the Great Wall of China. When the Tzarina died, Abram returned to court. Now back in favor since Peter the Great's daughter, Elizabeth—Abram's childhood friend—had been made empress, and she appointed him major general of the Imperial Russian Army and gifted him his own Mikhailovskoye estate in the Pskov Oblast (with more than a hundred "serfs"). Since he now had his own estate, he made a request to be recognized as a member of the nobility and was rewarded with his coat of arms, an elephant above the letters FVMMO—possibly a version of the Kotoko native African word for "homeland" or the initials of the Latin phrase *Fortuna Vitam Meam Mutavit Omnino*, "fortune has changed my life entirely."

After an unhappy first marriage, Abram found love with a Swedish noblewoman, Christina Regina Sioberg, and they had ten children together. Their oldest son, Ivan, also had an impressive military career.

In 1756, Abram was appointed Chief Military Engineer and, three years later, became General-in-Chief, the highest rank he could achieve. He spent his later years in retirement at his estate.

Abram died in St. Petersburg on 14 May 1781, aged around 85, having lived the most extraordinary life. Unsurprisingly, his great-grandson, the celebrated Russian writer Alexander Pushkin, was inspired to write about his experiences in his (unfinished) novel, *The Moor of Peter the Great.*

8

JEMMY - THE STONO REBEL

Jemmy was an enslaved person thought to have been born in the Kingdom of Kongo (now a part of Angola) around 1730. Little is known of his early life, but he was sold to or captured by the British Royal African Company and shipped to South Carolina.

Many of the Kongo's people had been converted to Christianity by Portuguese colonists, and although Jemmy was a Roman Catholic, he also held traditional Kongo beliefs. As a child growing up in West Africa, he had learned military skills and tactics, using pistols and muskets, from the Europeans, and he spoke Portuguese, which had become the language of trade and negotiation in his country.

It is possible that Jemmy fought in the civil wars that raged during the early part of the 18th Century and ended up dividing the Kingdom of Kongo and that he had a knowledge of farming rice before he was shipped to

South Carolina as when he arrived, he was put to work on a plantation as a skilled laborer.

Throughout the 1730s, several enslaved workers on the English plantations in South Carolina escaped to the neighboring Spanish-owned state of Florida. This inflamed tensions between the two colonists to such an extent that the Security Act legislation was passed in Carolina. This legislation included a rule that all white men were to carry firearms to church on Sundays, a time when they had always been unarmed and so the best time for laborers to take a chance on breaking free.

On 9 September 1739, it is unclear how long Jemmy had been in America. However, he and twenty of his fellow plantation workers had had enough of the long hours, menial work, and harsh punishments. They had been working by the Stono River, and before daybreak, Jemmy led them to the nearby Hutchinson store, from which they stole guns and ammunitions and then killed the two men guarding the store. They left and attacked the house owned by a plantation overseer named Godfrey and burned down his home, killing him, his son, and his daughter.

Demanding their freedom with shouts of protest, Jemmy and his band headed for the Wallace Tavern. They spared the innkeeper but killed his neighbors and some twenty other white people. They gathered more guns and weapons and then made their way south.

As they marched, more enslaved plantation workers joined them. When they reached the Edisto River, plantation owners and English town officials arrived to fight back and quickly put a stop to the uprising. They killed fourteen of the rebels, but several managed to escape into the woods and made their way to St. Augustine, Florida. Those they captured were executed or sold off to the West Indies. Jemmy was probably one of those killed, although this was not documented.

After the Stono Rebellion, as it became known, the South Carolina authorities recognized the need to improve conditions for the enslaved workers, not for any particular concern for their welfare but to help prevent further uprisings. Slave masters were to be disciplined for expecting the laborers to work over long hours or beating them without "good reason."

A school was founded for enslaved people to learn Christian teachings. With a current population in South Carolina consisting of more Black people than white, the shipping of enslaved people to the state was limited—again, for fear of rebellion—with the rule that there should be one white overseer for every ten enslaved Black workers. Furthermore, to keep better control of the workforce, an act was passed in 1740 that introduced strict rules that prohibited enslaved people from growing their own food, meeting together in groups, earning their own money, or learning to read.

The Stono Rebellion was South Carolina's largest and bloodiest uprising by enslaved people. Despite their cries for liberty and freedom, it resulted in even greater restrictions and suffering for the plantation workers at the hands of their cruel and ruthless overseers.

9

PHILLIS WHEATLEY - PIONEER POET

The *Phillis,* a slave transport ship, docked in Boston Harbor on 20 August 1761, packed with enslaved people. Among them was a little girl, aged about seven, who had been captured in Gambia. It was strange that she was there at all, as the slave trader had wanted to fill the ship with "prime boys" who would fetch him a good price. Thus, this poor little girl, wrapped in a dirty carpet, was a particularly sad and lonely figure.

She was taken to the slave market where Susanna Wheatley, the wife of a wealthy Boston merchant, was in need of a servant to help look after her in her older years. She was so moved by the "humble and modest demeanor and interesting features of the little stranger" that she bought her, despite several strong and fit, more suitable women being available that day.

Since the girl had no name, the Wheatleys called her "Phillis" after the ship that had brought her to Boston and decided to give her an education. The young girl proved extremely intelligent, and within sixteen months of her arrival in America, she had read the Bible, several classical Greek and Latin texts, and a great deal of English literature. She was also fascinated by geography and astronomy.

At the age of fourteen, Phillis began to write. Her poem *On Being Brought from Africa to America* gives a remarkable insight into her feelings about slavery. Although she expresses gratitude for her "Christian redemption," she also calls for white Christians to be held to account.

In 1770, she published *An Elegiac Poem, on the Death of the Celebrated Divine George Whitefield*, devoted to a well-known British evangelist. The quality of her writing and the story of the young poet made it an international success, and two years later, aged twenty, she was ready to publish a book of her poetry.

A committee of eighteen of Boston's leading officials and academics met to discuss whether Phillis, as an enslaved woman, was capable of writing poetry. After "examining" her, they decided that she was indeed and gave her a signed letter, addressed "to the public," giving her permission.

Phillis traveled to London, accompanied by Susanna's son, Nathaniel Wheatley, to publish her book, *Poems on Various Subjects, Religious, and Moral.* As the author, she was credited as "Phillis Wheatley, Negro Servant to Mr. John Wheatley, of Boston." The book was extremely well received. One of her poems described how she felt about her capture and people who owned enslaved people when

Britain was waking up to the need to abolish the shameful slave trade. It hit a nerve, with several public figures calling for Phillis to be given her freedom.

During her time in England, Susanna Wheatley fell ill, and Phillis returned to Boston to be at her side. Her British supporters were concerned for her welfare. Had she consented to leave? However, on 18 October 1773, Phillis wrote to tell them she had been freed.

Some historians believe that Phillis had only agreed to return to the Wheatleys on the condition that they would release her and that, perhaps, her reason for publishing her poetry was to gain her freedom.

After Susanna's death in 1774, Phillis—now a free woman —began to make her views known. She condemned owners of enslaved African people, comparing them to the Egyptians and persecuting the Hebrews in the Old Testament of the Bible.

During the American Revolution, she hoped that the war would release Black people from slavery and highlighted the hypocrisy of the people who said they were fighting for freedom while they owned enslaved people.

In 1778, Phillis married John Peters, a free Black man who owned a grocery shop in Boston. She also began preparing her second book of poetry for publication, this time under her new name, Phillis Peters. Unfortunately, John's business suffered badly after the war, and when he faced prosecution for his debts, he and Phillis fled from Boston.

The couple had three children, but unfortunately, all of them died. When John tried to start a new business, his debts caught up with him, and he was sent to prison. He was probably there when Phillis died at the age of (around) thirty-one, in childbirth, on 5 December 1784. She had been working in a laundry, scrubbing clothes, making ends meet, as well as working on her poetry.

Although Phillis never published her second book, she made a unique contribution to American literature. Her poems reflected a great sense of pride in her African heritage, and because she often wrote about religion and her spiritual beliefs, Protestants in America and England particularly enjoyed her work.

Through her poems, she was a shining light for the abolitionist cause, helping to convince the public, which had long been ignorant, that African Americans were capable of being intelligent, creative, and artistic and were both worthy of education and were just as able to contribute to art and culture as anyone else.

10

PRINCE ESTABROOK - FIGHTING FOR FREEDOM

The American Revolutionary War was an epic war that led to the foundation of the sovereign United States of America. The struggle began in 1765 when thirteen of Britain's North American colonies began to make a political stand against unpopular taxes and demanded the same rights as other British people. By 1775, the situation was quickly descending into a military conflict.

Many African Americans, free and enslaved, supported the Patriot (anti-British) cause, particularly in the northern colonies, where they had already joined private militias to help defend villages against attacks by Native Americans. These militiamen were well-trained soldiers, well able to use weapons, and knowledgeable about military tactics. Because they took pride in their readiness to fight at a minute's notice, they became known as "minutemen."

On the morning of 19 April 1775, an advanced guard of 240 British soldiers arrived at Lexington, a town in

Massachusetts, with the intention of seizing guns and ammunition to use against the threat posed by these armed minutemen.

At the Buckman Tavern in Lexington, however, a group of minutemen that had been hastily assembled after the midnight rider Paul Revere (one of a small band of patriots who raced ahead to warn their comrades of the British army's movements) had brought news that the enemy was marching west, to Lexington.

One of these minutemen was a man named Prince Estabrook. His parents had been enslaved African American people owned by Benjamin Estabrook. Under the laws of that time, he was also enslaved to Benjamin Estabrook from his birth, thought to be around 1740.

The Battle of Lexington was all over in about ten minutes. The smartly attired British army, in their red jackets, encountered around eighty minutemen at the North Bridge of Lexington. The Americans, commanded by Captain John Parker, a veteran who had fought alongside the British in earlier wars, were not in uniform. Mostly farmers and laborers, they were armed with muskets and weapons more commonly used for hunting.

John Parker said to his men, "Stand your ground; don't fire unless fired upon, but if they mean to have war, let it begin here." As the British arrived, one soldier fired a shot (no one is really sure whether it was a minuteman or one of the soldiers), and the British made their attack and fired at their enemy, then charged at them with their bayonets raised. Eight of the Massachusetts men were killed and several more wounded, including Prince Estabrook, who had been hit in the shoulder by musket fire. The British soldiers only suffered one casualty, and although they overcame the Patriots, this was the start of a long war, which they would ultimately lose.

Prince Estabrook recovered from his wound and continued his career as a minuteman. He fought with Captain Parker again, this time in Cambridge, in 1775. Later that same year, he served with Colonel Jonathan Reed's regiment at Fort Ticonderoga, the first offensive victory for the American forces of the war. He then fought at Cambridge once more, this time with Colonel Eleazer Brook's regiment, before joining a pool of men raised to reinforce George Washington's Continental Army. He joined Colonel John Greaton's regiment in 1782, then Colonel Michael Jackson's regiment in 1783.

The Continental Army was disbanded in 1783 after the Treaty of Paris formally ended the war, and Prince returned to Lexington a free man. It is not at all clear when he had been given his freedom, and it is believed that he continued to work for the Estabrooks but as a paid employee. Just as in his early life, little is known of his later years. There are no records that he ever married or had children, but it is believed that after Benjamin Estabrook's death, Prince moved to Ashby, Massachusetts, and continued to work for Nathan, Benjamin's son.

Prince died, aged around ninety, in 1830 and was laid to rest in the First Unitarian Universalist Church of Ashby burial ground. A hundred years later, a headstone was placed on his grave with a ceremony in which he was commemorated as "a brave defender of American liberty," very much at odds with the years he spent as an enslaved man. In more recent years, a bronze plaque near the Buckman Tavern in Lexington honors Prince Estabrook and the thousands of other African Americans who fought for both sides in the American Revolutionary War.

And now back to

THE
1800'S -
1900'S

11

VICENTE GUERRERO - MEXICAN REVOLUTIONARY

Vicente Ramón Guerrero Saldaña was born in Tixtla on 9 August 1782 into a family of African-American heritage. His father owned a successful mule freight business. After being educated by private teachers, the young Vicente began working in the family firm as a muleteer, a job that involved some traveling. Vicente met many different people and learned how many Mexican people were starting to look toward removing the Spanish from their country and independence for their country.

Vicente's father, Juan Pedro Guerrero, supported Spanish rule. On one occasion, he wanted to present his son's sword to the visiting Viceroy of New Spain, but Vicente refused, saying, "The will of my father is for me sacred, but my fatherland is first."

A failed attempt to overthrow the Spanish by Miguel Hidalgo, celebrated as the "father of Mexican independence," inspired Vicente to join the growing independence movement. In 1810, he fought alongside José María Morelos, an inspirational priest and freedom fighter.

The battles for independence were hard fought. Thousands of Mexicans lost their lives fighting both for and against the Spanish between 1810 and 1821. Vicente, despite having had no experience as a soldier, quickly proved himself on the battlefield with a natural flair for warfare. Morelos made him a captain and arranged for him to learn how to manufacture gunpowder, as well as teach him military tactics and strategies.

Vicente was able to put his new skills and studies into practice at the Capture of Oaxaca in 1812 and was promoted to the rank of lieutenant colonel. Morelos then sent him to the southern coastal regions, where he fought in the conquests of Puerto Escondido, Santa Cruz de Huatulco, and the Taking of Acapulco.

He supported independence forces making raids in his hometown of Mixteca, and the cause seemed to be making some headway until, in 1815, Morelos was captured and executed. Afterward, his supporters quickly fell into disarray. Vicente, however, had other ideas and pushed ahead, determined they would succeed. Even when the Spanish Viceroy, Juan Ruiz de Apodaca, tried to persuade Vicente to drop the cause, offering him a great deal of money, he would not give it up.

By the 1820s, Vicente's fight gathered momentum when new liberal laws that had been introduced in Spain looked likely to be enforced in the Spanish colonies. The ruling classes in Mexico were very concerned that these laws could ruin them, and they came to the idea that independence would actually suit them better. The Viceroy made another attempt to talk Vicente into backing down and sent his representative Agustín de Iturbide with the offer of a pardon. However, Iturbide decided to change sides, and it was with him that Vicente drafted the Iguala plan that proclaimed Mexico's independence from Spain, Roman Catholicism as the official religion, and equality for all inhabitants of Mexico, regardless of their birthplace.

With their plan for government, Vicente and Iturbide marched their forces on Mexico City and arrived in September 1821 to a hero's welcome. They proclaimed independence and sent a letter to the King of Spain, Ferdinand VII, notifying him that the state was no longer under Spanish rule but inviting him to provide a member of the royal family to serve as the new country's monarch.

The King rejected this proposal, so Iturbide was named Emperor of Mexico and ruled from 1822 to 1823, a period known as the First Mexican Empire. However, Vicente did not support his rulership and fought alongside his supporters, intent on Mexico being ruled by a Republican government.

In 1828, the presidential elections ended in chaos, and Vicente, by then regarded as the popular folk hero of the independence movement, was appointed President.

He set about introducing his reforms, the first being the complete abolition of slavery in Mexico. Slavery had already been banned by the Spanish authorities in 1818, and with some states already prohibiting the sale of enslaved people, by 16 September 1829, when Vicente's law was introduced, the practice had all but died out in the country. He also brought in other social changes: public schools, liberal trade development, and an overhaul of land titles. However, the years of struggling for independence had been expensive, and the Mexican economy could not support his ambitions.

He managed to fight off a Spanish attempt to re-conquer Mexico at the Battle of Tampico, but just seven months into his presidency, his enemies drove him out. He gathered his supporters to try and regain power, but he was captured in Acapulco and, on 14 February 1831, executed by a firing squad in Cuilapam.

It has been said that Vicente faced such strong opposition to his presidency due to his African heritage and that he was executed, rather than exiled, as a warning to help prevent other people that the ruling classes considered inferior from their ambitions to govern the country.

Vicente became a martyr to his causes, and he is remembered for his fight for equal rights for the people of Mexico, even describing him as the "greatest man of color to ever live."

12

GEORGE "CRUM" SPECK - MR. CHIPS

Great—and life-changing—inventions are often created by accident. That is exactly the case in (what is believed to be) the creation of the first potato chip.

It was George Speck, born on 15 July 1824 to an African-American father, Abraham Speck, and a Native American mother, Diana Tull, of the Huron Tribe, who is credited with inventing the savory snack. However, it is also possible that it might have been his sister, Catherine "Kate" Speck.

As a youngster, George worked as a guide in the Adirondack Mountains of New York, and he was an expert animal trapper, adept at snaring deer and wild ducks. But in 1853, he started work preparing meals at Moon's Lake House, a plush resort on the Saratoga River, where wealthy New Yorkers enjoyed taking their vacations.

It was at Moon's Lake House that George would first become known as "Crum." A rich patron (possibly Cornelius Vanderbilt, the shipping and railroad magnate) could never remember George's last name and took to calling him Crum, sending waiters to ask "Crum" for particular dishes for him. George quite liked the name, saying, "At least a crumb is bigger than a speck!" And it stuck.

George's marvelous invention occurred when a particularly annoying patron sent a plate of French fried potatoes back to the kitchen, telling the servers to let Crum know they were too soft, thick, and bland. George disagreed. Having had quite enough of this fussy diner, he decided to teach him a lesson. George took some new potatoes and sliced them as thinly as he possibly could— so fine he could see through them. He then fried them until they were golden and crispy. No one could ever say they were soft! Then, before serving, he over-salted them, sat back as they left the kitchen, and waited for the customer's inevitable howl of rage.

But nothing happened! The picky customer absolutely loved them. The Saratoga chip (or "potato crunch" was born! They quickly became hugely popular, and Cary Moon, the resort owner, had them served in cones and boxes so customers could take them away. Soon, they were just as popular as peanuts and candy in Saratoga.

In 1860, George bought a building on Storey Hill in Malta, New York, and opened his own restaurant called "Crum's." It was a great success. He always tried to use local produce, and he took pride in personally overseeing every dish. There was always a basket of his chips on every table, and his customers loved them. Kate, his sister, worked alongside him and, in her later years, suggested that it was actually she who, having accidentally dropped some potato shavings into the fryer, had invented them.

Either way, the Speck family never patented their idea. After his death in 1914, fast food companies saw an opportunity and made billions of dollars in mass producing and selling the ever-popular snacks. Crum and Kate's families never saw a penny, nor were the inventors ever given any real credit for their discovery.

13

HARRIET TUBMAN - AN AMERICAN ICON

Harriet Tubman had the most extraordinary life. Despite the most difficult start, she is recognized as one of the most inspirational and tenacious women of her time and a role model for anyone fighting against injustice and persecution.

She was born Araminta Ross in March 1822 to enslaved parents in Dorchester County, Maryland. She had eight brothers and sisters—all born on the property of the family that owned her parents. Harriet's mother, Rit, tried her best to keep the family together, but three of her daughters were sold, and they never saw them again. So when her youngest son was to be sold, Rit, with the help of the Black free and enslaved community, hid the little boy. Finally, the enslaver arrived to take him, but Rit refused to let him go and threatened to split the white man's head open if he tried. The enslaver left, and the sale never happened, with the young Harriet seeing the power of resistance.

At the age of five or six, Harriet started working as a nursemaid, caring for a baby and rocking its cradle while it slept. If the baby cried, Harriet was whipped. One day, she recalled being whipped five times before breakfast, and these lashes were savage, leaving scars that would remain with her throughout her life. She did other jobs on the plantations, such as checking muskrat traps, driving oxen, and hauling logs as soon as she was strong enough.

One day, Harriet was accidentally hit in the head by a heavy metal weight that a slave overseer was throwing at a laborer trying to escape. She later said it broke her skull, and she was left alone, unconscious and bleeding, at the enslavers' house for two days with no medical attention. Afterward, she suffered from painful headaches and seizures. She also had visions that she believed were messages from God, which helped her develop a deep and passionate spiritual faith.

Harriet never received any education other than her mother telling her Bible stories. She found she could not accept the teachings of white preachers at her local church who told the enslaved congregation that they should accept their situation with humility and obedience. She liked the Old Testament stories of God punishing those who offended him and enslaved people rising up against their oppressors.

In 1844, Harriet married a free Black man, John Tubman, but this did not change her own enslaved status. It was then that she changed her name to Harriet, probably because she was planning to escape.

The enslaver wanted to sell her but struggled to find a buyer due to her health problems after the head injury. Harriet seethed with anger and prayed that God would strike him down, and when he died a week later, she felt bad about it. The situation for the Ross family worsened as his widow started to sell off her husband's enslaved people with no interest in helping the families stay together.

When Harriet and two of her brothers were sold to a neighboring plantation, they took the opportunity to escape. This was a short-lived attempt as the men quickly decided they should turn back since they were missing their wives and families and forced Harriet to return with them.

In the autumn of 1849, Harriet broke free again—this time without her brothers. She was helped by the "Underground Railroad," a network of freed and enslaved Black people and white abolitionists, such as the Quakers. Under the care of these "conductors," Harriet was passed from place to place, often hidden out of sight since rewards were paid to people who captured runaways.

Finally, Harriet was in Pennsylvania. She said she felt like she was "in heaven" and could hardly believe she was the same person. She started working odd jobs to save money so that her family could also make their escapes. In 1850, she was able to help her niece and her children (who were due to be sold separately) get to Pennsylvania.

The following year, she returned to Maryland to act as a guide on the Underground Railroad and helped her younger brother and several others to escape. She was disappointed to find that her husband had married someone else. However, she still continued her work as a guide, leading some seventy enslaved people to freedom in thirteen expeditions and arranging the escape of as many again. It was dangerous; there were many times when she might have been recognized and captured, but her quick wits, ingenuity, determination, faith in God, and the revolver she carried gave her the confidence to continue. She spent eight years as a conductor on the Underground Railroad and was proud that she never lost any of her "passengers." One of her last missions was to rescue her aging parents who, despite having been freed, were at risk of being arrested for hiding a group of escapees. She guided them to St. Catherines in Canada, where a community of former enslaved people was developing.

In April 1858, Harriet joined John Brown's militant abolitionist movement and began to recruit others prepared to physically attack slaveholders in what was hoped would become a national rebellion, but on the day of the organized raid on Harpers Ferry in Virginia, she was sick and could not fight. John Brown, however, was captured and hanged, having been convicted of treason and murder.

Harriet bought a small farm near Auburn, New York, in 1859. It quickly became a shelter for her family and displaced Black people looking for a safe place to stay. The political and economic situation in America was beginning to collapse, and Harriet, having had a vision that the Civil War would lead to the abolition of slavery, readily supported the Union forces. She traveled to South Carolina and worked as an (unpaid) nurse caring for wounded and diseased Unionist soldiers and became a scout for Colonel James Montgomery, using the skills she had developed on the Underground Railroad to spy on the Confederate positions.

She was at the forefront of the raid at Combahee River, where she guided three steamboats of Black soldiers who attacked several plantations and set fire to them. The enslaved workers had been warned of the action by Harriet's network of spies and were all ready to leave. The enslavers tried to stop the exodus, but more than 750 formerly enslaved people, with hastily packed bags, babies in their arms, and some even carrying pigs, were crammed onto the steamboats that sailed away down the river. Harriet's role in the raid reached the newspapers, and "General Tubman" (as she had become known) is widely considered to have been the first woman to lead American troops in an armed assault.

After the Civil War, Harriet returned to her farm in Auburn and cared for her elderly parents, who had moved from Canada. She took in boarders, including Nelson Davis, a former soldier who had also been enslaved and worked as a bricklayer. He and Harriet fell in love and married on 18 March 1869. Their family was complete when they adopted a little girl, Gertie, in 1874.

Harriet always struggled financially. She was rarely paid for her services, and when she was widowed in 1888, she had to fight to receive a pension for Nelson's war service.

After slavery had been abolished, there were other causes she campaigned for. As a suffragist, she regularly attended meetings and even traveled to Boston and Washington, DC, to speak of her views about women's right to vote. She was also concerned about provisions for elderly Black people and raised funds for the "Harriet Tubman Home for the Aged," which almost bankrupted her.

In her final years, her old head injury gave her a lot of pain, and she persuaded a doctor at the Massachusetts General Hospital to operate, without anesthetic, to make her more comfortable. By 1911, she was very frail, and when a newspaper reported that she was "ill and penniless," many people donated money to help.

Harriet died, aged ninety, and was buried with semi-military honors at Fort Hill Cemetery in Auburn. She is remembered with great affection as a true heroine of civil rights and one of the most famous figures in American history.

14

JOHN BROWN - "AND HIS SOUL GOES MARCHING ON"

One name that cannot be overlooked in the American struggle for the abolition of slavery is that of John Brown. He was neither Black nor enslaved, but he could not stand by while his fellow man was brutally persecuted and subjugated.

John was born on 9 May 1800 in Torrington, Connecticut. His family moved to Ohio, where his father started a new tannery business near one of the main "stops" on the Underground Railroad (the route by which enslaved people were helped to escape to freedom). John's father was very sympathetic to the plight of these runaways, and Brown's home became a safe house for those making their escape on the Railroad.

John left home at sixteen to start his own business but struggled to make much success until 1833, when he found a partner and started up again, this time in Springfield, Massachusetts. By then, he was very involved in the abolitionist cause and had begun to believe that passive resistance would not bring an end to slavery and that a campaign of aggressive action was the only way to bring about change.

In 1850, he moved with his family to Timbuctoo, a farming community in the Adirondack region of New York. There, the wealthy Abolitionist Gerritt Smith had started to gift land to Black farmers, and that enabled them (as land or homeowners) the right to vote. John bought his own farm near Lake Placid and did what he could to help his Black neighbors.

By 1855, two of his sons had grown up and had their own families. Both fervent abolitionists relocated to the western territory that would become Kansas and told their father that some of the pro-slavery inhabitants had started to threaten abolitionists with violence. John traveled west to join them, wondering whether Kansas might become a state for free, former enslaved people if they could make enough of a stand.

John's sons were right to worry. A pro-slavery mob marched into the town of Lawrence on 21 May 1856 to attack the *Herald of Freedom* newspaper office, furious at its criticism of the pro-slavery government, destroying the printing presses and throwing the papers into the river. The next day, Republican Senator Charles Sumner of Massachusetts made an impassioned address in the US Senate condemning this "crime against Kansas," and afterward, on the floor of the House, Representative Preston S.

Brooks of South Carolina set upon him with his cane to beat him so badly, he was unable to return to his seat for three years.

John prepared to fight back. On the nights of 24–25 May, he took four of his sons and three other abolitionists, and they attacked and murdered five pro-slavery men at three different cabins at Pottawatomie Creek.

In the years that followed, the two sides launched violent raids and assaults on each other in, what has become known as, Bleeding Kansas. Around 55 people were killed in the confrontations, and as John's abolitionist cause gathered support, he traveled the country to speak to the people about the vile practice of slavery and raised money to arm his men.

Bleeding Kansas came to an end after the election of Abraham Lincoln in 1861. Kansas held elections and voted for a free state government, and it was no longer under the control of Missouri.

But by no means had John finished his fight to raise his country's consciousness. He began planning a raid that he hoped would start a widespread revolution and an end to slavery. He had the support of other abolitionists, including Harriet Tubman and Frederick Douglass, who agreed with his radical approach and promised to do what they could to help.

The target of his attack was to be the US military armory at Harpers Ferry in Virginia (now West Virginia). He recruited 22 men, including his sons, Owen and Watson, for the operation, and they trained with former soldiers who had joined John's movement.

On 16 October 1859, his men were struck with the capture of Colonel Lewis Washington (a distant relative of George Washington), whose family still enslaved people, and a raid on the armory. They needed to act quickly before officials in Washington learned of their uprising and sent soldiers to fight against them. So they stopped a Baltimore and Ohio railroad train heading for Washington from leaving the station to stop any passengers from raising the alarm when they arrived. During their efforts, however, a baggage handler ignored the orders shouted by John's men and was shot in the back and killed. Unfortunately, this casualty was a free Black man, exactly the sort of person these rebels were trying to support.

John took some of the railway workers captive and then let the train go, but as soon as he was able, the conductor told the Washington authorities what he had seen at Harpers Ferry, and they raised the alarm.

Meanwhile, the abolitionist rebels had captured several landowners, but the townspeople were growing impatient and began to fight back. The next morning, the local militia secured the bridge that crossed the Potomac River so that Brown's men would not be able to make an escape.

Then, they surrounded the armory and fired at John and his men inside. The rebels fired back and killed four, including the town's mayor. As more armed men arrived to support the militia, the rebels moved into the armory engine house, "John Brown's Fort."

During the standoff, the militia managed to free some of the captives. But when eight of the railroad workers were killed in the fighting, John began to realize his uprising could not continue and sent his son, Watson, to surrender on their behalf, but as he made his way to the militia, Watson was shot and died from his wounds soon after.

In the early evening of 17 October, reinforcements arrived from Washington under the command of Colonel Robert E. Lee, who marched his marines to Harpers Ferry. Colonel Lee tried to persuade John to surrender, but he refused. The marines then stormed the "fort" and took everyone, the abolitionist rebels and their captives, out alive.

John Brown was arrested and charged with treason against the Commonwealth of Virginia. He was tried at the courthouse at Charles Town and found guilty, and on 2 December 1859, he was hanged. His death was witnessed by Colonel Lee and the pro-slavery activist John Wilkes Booth, who would assassinate President Abraham Lincoln in 1865 after his government succeeded in abolishing slavery.

In 1856, John declared, "I have only a short time to live, only one death to die, and I will die fighting for this cause. There will be no peace in this land until slavery is done for." He became a martyr to the anti-slavery cause, and his actions at Harpers Ferry ultimately led to the Civil War, forcing the people of America to change their stance on slavery.

15

BLANCHE KELSO BRUCE - A POLITICAL TRAILBLAZER

The American Civil War, which was fought between the United States of America and the eleven southern states that made up the Confederate States of America, ended in 1865 with the Emancipation Proclamation, intended to put an end to slavery.

The period that followed, from 1861 until 1865, is known as the Reconstruction Era, a time when the United States rebuilt its great nation with the Confederate States fully integrated. Three amendments were added to the Constitution: the 13th abolished slavery, the 14th guaranteed all citizen's rights that were protected by the law, and the 15th prohibited discrimination on voting rights, regardless of "*race, color or previous condition of servitude.*" One of the conditions of the Confederate States joining the Union was that the former enslaved people would be guaranteed their human rights.

Despite these efforts, freed Black people in the southern states were subjected to the most appalling racism and violent attacks. The Bureau of Refugees, Freedmen, and Abandoned Lands (usually shortened to the "Freedmen's Bureau"), created by the government to oversee the move from slavery for the 4 million formerly enslaved people, did help to better the situation, with the US Army on hand to stop tensions from bubbling over.

The election of President Andrew Johnson in 1865, however, was a blow to the abolitionists and former enslaved people. For years, he had defended slavery as "inevitable," and once in office, he did what he could to limit the rights African Americans had been given.

One of these former enslaved men was Blanche Bruce. He had been born into slavery in 1841; his mother, Polly, had been served in the household of his father, a Virginia planter, Pettis Perkinson.

Blanche's father allowed him an education, but he only gained his freedom when he moved to Kansas at the start of the Civil War. There, he began to teach while studying at college and then worked as a porter on a steamboat. As the war drew to a close, he moved to Hannibal, Missouri, where he founded a school for Black children.

At the time of Reconstruction, Blanche bought a plantation in the Mississippi Delta and quickly amassed a great deal of money, and this enabled him to start a career in politics. He was elected sheriff in Bolivar County and stood for several other supervisory offices until, by 1870, he was sergeant-at-arms for the Mississippi State Senate.

In 1874, Blanche was elected to the US Senate to serve in the Upper House of Congress, and on 14 February 1879, he was the first African American—and the only formerly enslaved person—to preside over the Senate. He fought for fair treatment for Black and native Americans and pushed for Chinese immigrants to be given equal civil rights. But in the political climate of that time, a lot of his time in office was spent calling out fraud and corruption in federal elections.

During the Reconstruction Era, the Federal Government had authorized the founding of a bank for formerly enslaved people to help them become financially independent and stable; many of them had little understanding of managing money after years of slavery, but this Freedmen's Savings and Trust was mismanaged and, by 1874, it had collapsed. Blanche was chosen to chair the investigation into this scandal.

After leaving the Senate, President James Garfield appointed him Registrar of the Treasury, and at the Republican Convention of 1888, he received eleven votes for vice president. The following year, he became Recorder of Deeds for the District of Columbia and joined Howard University's Board of Trustees. He returned to his role in the Treasury in 1897.

Blanche died in 1898 in Washington, DC, at age fifty-seven. He is remembered as the first African American to be elected to the US Senate and serve a full term and, unquestionably, one of the most successful Black politicians of his time.

16

REBECCA LEE CRUMPLER - THE GOOD DOCTRESS

Any woman thinking about a career as a doctor in 19th Century America faced a seemingly impossible challenge. Women who had a vocation for medicine became nurses or midwives, so it is remarkable that one of the first female physicians was African American.

Rebecca Davis was born in 1831 in Christiana, Delaware. As a girl, she spent a lot of her time with her aunt, who devotedly cared for her sick neighbors and was an inspiration to her. In her later years, she wrote, *"Having been reared by a kind aunt in Pennsylvania, whose usefulness with the sick was continually sought, I early conceived a liking for, and sought every opportunity to be in a position to relieve the sufferings of others."*

In 1852, Rebecca married a widower, Wyatt Lee, who was a former enslaved plantation worker from Virginia who had a little boy, Albert. The family moved to Charles Town, Massachusetts, and Rebecca started nursing. At that time, there was no formal training or licensing, so

Rebecca learned her skills by assisting doctors in Boston and caring for the sick. Albert died when he was just seven years old, and this may well have been the reason for Rebecca's determination to become a doctor.

As the American Civil War began, so many soldiers needed treatment for their wounds that unique opportunities arose for women wanting to train in medicine. Rebecca was recommended to The New England Female Medical College by one of the doctors she had worked alongside, and her tuition fees were paid by the Wade Scholarship Fund, a bequest from the Ohio abolitionist Benjamin Wade.

Her medical training was interrupted when Wyatt developed tuberculosis. After Rebecca had cared for him until his death in 1863, she re-enrolled. After she had completed three years of coursework, a thesis, and a final oral exam, the school's board of trustees declared Rebecca Lee a Doctress of Medicine on 1 March 1864.

Rebecca's first patients were poor African-American women and children in Boston whom she knew could not afford to pay. She worked for the Freedmen's Bureau, treating Black people that white doctors had refused medical care, but she was subjected to appalling racism from her fellow physicians and often had to fight to get her prescriptions filled.

Rebecca married again to Arthur Crumpler on 24 May 1865 at Saint John, New Brunswick. Arthur had been enslaved and then served as a blacksmith for the Union Army in the Civil War at Fort Monroe, Virginia. The

Crumplers made their home at 20 Garden Street in Boston and were active members of the Twelfth Baptist Church, where Arthur was a trustee. They had a daughter, Lizzie, in 1870, but it is thought that she died young since they did not have a child living with them when they moved to Hyde Park, Massachusetts, in 1880, when Rebecca stopped practicing as a doctor.

In 1883, Rebecca compiled a book from the notes she had made during her career. *A Book of Medical Discourses* covered health advice for pregnancy, motherhood, and child health, and it is believed to be the first medical text written by an African-American author.

There are no known photographs or paintings of Rebecca. But in her later years, she was described in an article in the Boston Globe as being *"tall and straight, with light brown skin and grey hair"* and *"a very pleasant and intellectual woman and an indefatigable church worker..."*

Rebecca died on 9 March 1895, and Arthur died five years later. They were laid to rest side by side in unmarked graves in Fairview Cemetery until, in 2020, headstones were erected after a fundraising campaign.

17

ANTONIO MACEO - THE TITAN OF BRONZE

In the second half of the 19th century, the South American country of Cuba became increasingly frustrated with its position as a colony. It had been part of the Spanish Empire since 1521 and governed by the Viceroyalty of New Spain from Mexico City, so Cubans had little say over their lives and were forced to pay high taxes. On 25 October 1868, Carlos Mañuel de Céspedes gave the *Grito de Yara* ("The Cry of Yara") that signaled the start of the Ten Years' War, the fight for Cuban independence, in which more than 200,000 were killed.

One freedom fighter was Antonio Maceo. He was born in 1845 in Santiago de Cuba, the son of a free Black Venezuelan landowner who owned several farms in the eastern province. He became interested in the move to independence from an early age, and when he joined a Masonic lodge at the age of eighteen, he met others who longed for change.

Antonio and his brothers answered The Cry of Yara and prepared to fight. Antonio proved to be a natural, clever soldier and was soon promoted to commander, then, in January 1869, lieutenant colonel of the Liberation Army. He began a program of raids on the Spanish-owned sugar plantations to disrupt the harvests, free enslaved laborers, and enlist them into his army.

Although Antonio was extremely popular, some Cubans feared he was trying to create a Black state with himself as its head, so when there was resistance to liberating the laborers in the western provinces, Antonio had to postpone his raids. The Spanish called him the "lion," while the Cubans named him their "*Titan of Bronze*." The liberation army had other problems; money, weapons, and ammunition promised by Cuban exiles in the United States never arrived. With both sides failing to win the war, on 11 February 1878, the Peace of Zanjón was agreed upon.

Most Cuban generals signed the treaty, but Antonio would not accept its terms and vowed to fight on, leading what remained of the liberation army. He met the head of the Spanish forces to make his two demands: an end to slavery in Cuba and independence, but Marshal Arsenio Martínez Campos would not agree to them.

Antonio continued his fight, but it was hopeless. His army was exhausted and poorly equipped, so he traveled to Jamaica, then to New York to try and raise support and funds for his war, and then to the Dominican Republic, Honduras, and finally, Costa Rica, trying to organize a new rebellion. Disillusioned by the lack of support, he started a business growing tobacco and sugar.

In 1893, however, he was called on to help lead a final effort to overthrow the Spanish from Cuba, and in March 1895, he landed in Oriente Province, ready to battle. For three months, he fought bitterly against the Spanish until his troops were attacked near the small town of San Pedro in Havana, and Antonio was killed.

He had fought in 500 battles against the Spanish Empire forces, and although he would never see it, his actions helped to end Spain's domination over Cuba.

18

BOOKER T. WASHINGTON - TUSKEGEE TEACHER

On 5 April 1856, a little boy was born in a slave hut on the plantation of James Burroughs in South West Virginia, near Hale's Ford in Franklin County. His mother was Jane, an enslaved woman, and he never knew his father. He was known as Booker, with no other name.

Born into slavery, he and his siblings had a difficult childhood, and life was a constant struggle, but early in 1865, the atmosphere began to change. He recalled hearing more singing on the plantation, songs about the longing for freedom that continued long into the night. Then, one day, everything changed. *"A stranger (a US Officer, I presume) made a little speech and then read a rather long paper, the Emancipation Proclamation, I think. After the reading, we were told that we were all free and could go when and where we pleased. My mother, standing by my side, leaned over and kissed her children while tears of joy ran down her cheeks. She explained to us what it all meant, that this was the day for which she had been so long praying, but fearing she would never see."*

Jane took her children to Malden, West Virginia. Although free, they were desperately poor, and Booker, aged nine, started working at a salt furnace and then in a coal mine. He was, however, determined to get an education and enrolled at the Hampton Normal and Agricultural Institute in Virginia, which had been established for the education of freed people and their descendants, when he was sixteen. He took the name of his mother's husband, "Washington," and added the middle name "Taliaferro," which he discovered she had given him when he was born. To pay for his studies, he worked as a janitor there.

After he had graduated in 1875, he returned to Malden as a schoolteacher and, after finishing classes, taught adults in the evenings. He returned to his studies at Wayland Seminary, Washington, DC, and in 1879, joined the staff at Hampton.

In 1881, Booker was recommended to head a new school for African-American people to receive further education, the Tuskegee Normal and Industrial Institute, in Alabama. It began in a small, two-room building donated by the Butler Chapel AME Zion Church with no equipment and very little money, but Booker had a vision.

He believed that African-American people in the years that followed the Reconstruction Era had to focus on education, then finding self-reliance and security by developing their farming and industrial skills rather than fighting for full civil rights. In this way, Black people would gradually become wealthier and more cultured, breaking the divisions between them and the white ruling classes, and ultimately, an integrated society would emerge.

To this end, he acquired an old plantation where the students would build their new school, and they rolled up their sleeves and got to work. They constructed class-rooms and farm buildings from bricks they had made themselves, learning and developing skills as they worked. Booker's school aimed to prepare his students, men and women, to teach in the new schools and colleges being founded for Black people in the southern states.

As the Tuskegee School expanded and more courses and facilities were added, Booker's reputation grew. White politicians and public servants sought his opinion, and on 18 September 1895, he was invited to speak at the Atlanta Exposition in Washington. He said, in his speech, "*In all things that are purely social, we can be separate as the fingers, yet one as the hand in all things essential to mutual progress.*" Some Black activists, however, disagreed with his outlook and were unhappy with him being a spokesperson for African Americans, arguing that action for civil rights was needed immediately as discrimination and segregation were becoming a way of life for Black people in the Southern States of America.

Most Black people, however, were more comfortable with Booker's approach and could see that he influenced the country's leaders. President William McKinley and many other respected officials visited his Tuskegee School, and he received honorary degrees from Harvard University and Dartmouth College.

After heading his school for thirty years, Booker died. He published several books, including his autobiography, *Up From Slavery*, in 1901, which explains his belief that there is dignity to be found in hard work and that it was through education that he was able to achieve such social status. *"Success is to be measured not so much by the position that one has reached in life as by the obstacles which he has overcome while trying to succeed."*

19

PHILIP B. DOWNING - POSTER BOY

Philip Bell Downing was born in Providence, Rhode Island, on 22 March 1857. His father, a business owner, had been a well-known abolitionist, and the Downing family relocated several times when Philip was growing up. They moved from Providence to Newport and later to Washington, DC, where George Downing became the dining room manager at the House of Representatives.

Philip and his five brothers and sisters soon became aware of the difficulties families faced when they moved into a new house, street, or state and all the paperwork that needed to be completed each time.

Philip moved to Massachusetts around 1880 and married Evangeline, with whom he had two children. He started a long career as a clerk with the Custom House in Boston. Despite being a busy family man, Philip always thought about how everyday problems might be solved or made easier. He put his ideas on paper and then applied for patents from the US Patent Office.

On 17 June 1890, his application for a *"new and useful improvement in street-railway switches"* was approved. This allowed the switches to be opened and closed by the brakeman from the platform on a streetcar, and this invention was the basis for the light switch.

His next patent, on 27 October 1891, was for the street letterbox. This was a clever idea that he had been thinking about since his childhood. He had never forgotten seeing his parents having to travel to post offices, in all weather, to send their mail, and sometimes, these post offices were a long, long way from their home.

His idea was for a street mailbox that people could pop their mail into, and then mail carriers would open and empty them, then take the letters to the post office to be processed—simple.

Philip's boxes were constructed from metal and stood on four legs. They had self-closing, hinged doors to protect the mail from theft or bad weather, and he even worked out exactly where they should be positioned on the pavement—six to eight inches away from the curb edge. Later that same year, he patented an additional feature to the mailbox, a chute to help mail carriers quickly remove the contents. The new system was a great success.

He had other patents awarded: a device with a roller and a little water reservoir to moisten envelopes and a notepad specifically designed for clerical workers sitting at desks, but it is the postboxes standing proudly on the streets of America, despite some minor modifications, still as their inventor intended, that remain clever Mr. Downing's legacy.

DR. GEORGE GRANT - BOSTON TEE PARTY

George Grant was born in Oswego, New York in 1847. As a youngster, he found a job as an errand boy for a local dentist and eventually became an assistant in his laboratory.

At nineteen, George left Oswego for Boston and worked as a dental assistant until, in 1868, he was accepted at the new Harvard Dental School. He graduated with honors three years later—the second African American to qualify there.

He remained at Harvard to continue his specialist work, treating patients who had defects on the roofs of their mouths and often found it difficult to eat or speak. He made special inserts, individually formed for each person, called "oblate palates," which were a great help to them. This work became well known and respected by dentists throughout America and overseas.

When he married and had a family, George left Harvard to set up his own dental practice in Boston and enjoyed a game of golf when he wasn't working. In fact, he became such a passionate golfer, and he had a meadow golf course built next to his house at Arlington Heights. Even when the family moved to Beacon Hill, George returned to his old golf course whenever he could.

Despite his love of the game, George found the process of teeing up the ball incredibly frustrating. He wanted to get on with the game and swing his clubs, but having to scrabble about in the dirt, pinching and molding a bit of sand to make a raised area for his ball eighteen times a game was spoiling it for him.

It was so annoying that George came up with an idea to sort out the problem, then applied for and received a patent (number 638,920) for his solution, a golf tee.

His invention was a pointed wooden peg attached to a rubber tube with a molded cup on the top where the ball could rest off the ground, ready for the golfer's swing.

George had little interest in his idea becoming a business —he was first and foremost a dentist—so he just asked local tradespeople to manufacture his tees and handed them out to friends and golf partners.

Others have claimed the invention of the golf tee, but George was the first to hold a patent. In 1991 (almost a century after he had patented his design and eighty years after his death), the US Golf Association officially recognized his contribution to the game and his place in sporting history.

From

1900 - 1950...

21

MARY KENNER - PROBLEM SOLVER

Mary Beatrice Davidson was born into a family of inventors in 1912. The Davidsons of North Carolina were constantly looking at ways of improving everyday life or finding simple solutions to problems.

Mary's grandfather had invented a tricolor light signal for trains. Her father had patented a portable clothing press, small enough to fit in a suitcase. Mildred, her sister, designed board games for a living.

Inventing began early for Mary. At the age of six, she was working on a self-oiling hinge to stop a door from squeaking, and then she turned her attention to the possibility of adding a sponge to the tip of an umbrella to help absorb some of the excess rainwater.

When the family moved to Washington, DC, aged twelve, she enjoyed nothing more than visiting the US Patent and Trademark Office to see the patents that had been awarded—and to check whether anyone had solved the problems she was working on.

After she graduated from Dunbar High School in 1931, Mary was offered a place at Howard University, but as she couldn't afford to complete her studies and, without any college degree or professional training, she became a florist and worked hard. She eventually opened four flower shops in the Washington area.

During the Second World War, she found work supporting the war effort at the Census Bureau and then at the General Accounting Office. She also chaperoned young women at dances held at military bases in Washington DC and met her first husband, a soldier, at one of them. Like a lot of wartime romances, it wasn't to last, and they divorced in 1950. The following year, she married again; her second husband was the heavyweight boxer James "Jabbo" Kenner. They moved to McLean, Virginia, and fostered five boys.

Mary never stopped inventing; her best-known idea was an adjustable sanitary belt. Women had long struggled to find comfortable aids to wear during menstruation, and as fashions changed and more fitted clothes were being worn, there was a real need for better products. Mary's design included an inbuilt, moisture-proof pocket, and she was granted her patent in 1956.

Soon afterward, she was contacted by the Sonn-Nap-Pack Company, which expressed an interest in manufacturing this invention and told her they were sending a representative to discuss the possibility. Mary wrote, *"I was so jubi-*

lant... I saw houses, cars, and everything about to come my way." But it wasn't to be; *"Sorry to say, when they found out I was Black, their interest dropped. The representative went back to New York and informed me the company was no longer interested."*

Although it was a disappointment, Mary continued to develop her ideas. She and Mildred received a joint patent for their toilet tissue holder, and Mary also designed a back-washing device that could be attached to a bathroom (or shower) wall. In 1959, when Mildred became sick and disabled from multiple sclerosis, Mary invented a carrier attachment for her walker.

Mary died on 13 January 2006 at the age of 93. Although she received little recognition for her inventions during her lifetime, she received more patents (five in total) than any other Black woman in the United States of America.

22

GARRETT MORGAN - "THE BLACK EDISON"

Garrett Augustus Morgan was an inventor who saved countless lives with two revolutionary devices: his traffic signal and smoke hood.

He was born in Paris, Kentucky, in 1917, the seventh of eleven children. His mother was a former enslaved woman, and his father—also a freed enslaved person—was the son of the famous Confederate general, John H. Morgan.

When he was fourteen, Garrett moved to Cincinnati, Ohio, looking for work. Being technically and mechanically minded, he was hired to repair sewing machines at a large clothing manufacturer. However, Garrett was not content with simply fixing them and invented a belt fastener and a zigzag stitch attachment that could be attached to the sewing machines.

In 1907, Garrett opened his own sewing machine shop in Cleveland and then, with his wife, opened a ladies' clothes store. These both proved very successful and allowed him the time to work on developing and patenting his ideas and inventions.

His first patent was for hair products. While he was working on finding the chemicals best suited for cleaning sewing machine needles, he noticed a compound that relaxed the curly hair on a piece of pony skin. After straightening his neighbor's dog's fur and his own hair, he knew he had something. He also developed other hair care products, including a hair-growing cream, black hair oil, and a comb to help with the straightening process.

Garrett was one of the founders and the first treasurer of the National Association for the Advancement of Colored People (NAACP) in 1909, a civil rights organization that continues to fight for equal rights for African-American people in the United States to this day.

In 1914, he formed the National Safety Device Company after being awarded a patent for his "smoke hood." A few years earlier, a fire had killed 146 workers in a clothing factory in New York, most of them young female immigrants. Garrett, having had experience in similar workplaces, wondered if lives could have been saved when he learned that most had died from smoke inhalation. In a fire, smoke and fumes rise with the hot air and form a kind of toxic canopy around the height of a person's head. He developed a head covering with a long tube that dangled much lower so the wearer could inhale the breathable air from below the smoke and fumes. It has been said that he was inspired after seeing a group of elephants in a hot circus tent sticking their trunks outside in an effort to cool down.

Not only was Garrett a clever inventor, but he had some innovative marketing ideas, too. He took his hoods around the country and often hired a white actor to pose as the inventor, knowing people were reluctant to trust a product developed by a Black person. He also disguised himself as a Native American character he invented from the Walpole Island Reserve in Canada, "Big Chief Mason." He would make a fire from tar, manure, and poisonous chemicals inside an enclosed tent. Once the smoke was thick, black, and smelt terrible, Garrett, as Big Chief Mason, would put on a hood, enter the tent, and stay there for twenty minutes. These demonstrations worked well, and he sold hoods to the fire departments of several hospitals and factories throughout the country.

The Cleveland Fire Department was treated to a private demonstration and bought several units. The Fire Chief was impressed at its simplicity and how easily and quickly it could be used compared with the oxygen masks they were using at that time.

On 24 July 1916, there was a major disaster in Ohio—an explosion in a tunnel being excavated for the Cleveland Waterworks. After two attempts to rescue the workers in the tunnels had failed, someone remembered Garrett's demonstration, and a messenger was sent for him. It was the middle of the night, and he gathered together as many hoods as he and his brother, Frank, could carry, and still in their pajamas, they hurried to the rescue site.

A lot of the people there weren't convinced by Garrett's device, but he, Frank, and two others went inside the tunnel wearing hoods and returned carrying some of the rescuers who had become victims to the effects of the fumes from the explosion, still alive. They went in again and again, managing to rescue a total of eight men, and then returned to retrieve the bodies of those who had perished. Despite the success of his invention, it could not completely prevent the wearer from inhaling some poisonous fumes, and Garrett suffered from the effects of the rescue for many years.

In the following weeks, Garrett found his role in the rescue completely overlooked by the newspapers and city officials, and he felt sure this was because he was Black. Awards and commendations for bravery were given to several of the people who had been at the tunnel, but there was no mention of Garrett and his brother. Some of the townspeople agreed; Victor M. Sincere of the Bailey Company, presenting him with an award, said, *"Your deed should serve to break down the shafts of prejudice with which you struggle. And is sure to be the beacon of light of those that follow you in the battles of life."* In 1917, the city of Cleveland awarded him with a gold medal, studded with diamonds, as a rather belated mark of gratitude for his heroism.

In the wake of the disaster, order requests for smoke hoods came flooding in from all over America, but some orders from the Southern States were withdrawn when they learned that Garrett was African American.

In 1923, after witnessing a dreadful collision between a horse-drawn carriage and a motor car at a crossing, Garrett had another idea for public safety and returned to his drawing board. He designed a traffic light system with folding arms that could be raised halfway to give a warning option as well as the traditional "stop" and "go." This would eventually become the yellow/amber light on traffic lights today. He patented his idea in the United States, Canada, and Great Britain and eventually sold the rights to General Electric for a great deal of money— enough to buy 250 acres of land in Wakeman, Ohio, and build a country club for African Americans, complete with a dance hall and a party suite.

Garrett was a brilliant inventor. He knew his worth and liked to call himself "The Black Edison." He died after a long illness in 1963 and had been blind for the last fifteen years of his life. Despite his great achievements and successes, the racism he faced had dogged him throughout his career. In his own words, "*I am a graduate from the school of hard knocks and cruel treatment.*" Since his death, his contribution to public safety has been recognized with streets, schools, and water plants named in his honor in Ohio and other states across America.

23

SISTER ROSETTA THARPE - THE ORIGINAL SOUL SISTER

In the years before Chuck Berry, Elvis Presley, and Little Richard delighted audiences with rock 'n' roll, the genre of music that evolved from African-American jazz, gospel, and blues traditions, Sister Rosetta Tharpe, also known as the Godmother of Rock 'n' Roll, had performed and recorded the songs that would set them on their way.

She was born Rosetta Nubin on 20 March 1915 in Arkansas, where her parents were cotton pickers. Her mother, Katie Bell Nubin, was a singer, a mandolin player, and a deaconess-missionary for the Church of God in Christ (COGIC), a Holiness-Pentecostal church founded in 1897 in Memphis, Tennessee.

The church was an important foundation for Katie and Rosetta. It encouraged its followers to express their devotion through rhythmic musical singing and dancing, and Little Rosetta Nubin, at the age of six, performed with her mother with a traveling evangelical group.

In the 1920s, Katie and Rosetta settled in Chicago, Illinois, where they continued to perform at the COGIC Robert's Temple. Rosetta had amassed quite a following, and people loved her surprisingly powerful mezzo-soprano voice and her unique style of playing her electric guitar, melodic and full of subtle slides.

At age 19, Rosetta married Thomas Thorpe, a COGIC preacher who often accompanied her and Katie when they traveled to perform. The marriage didn't last long, but Rosetta quite liked her married name, though she changed it a little and performed under the stage name Sister Rosetta Tharpe.

In 1938, she moved to New York City with her mother and started her recording career with four tracks for Decca on 31 October: "Rock Me," "That's All," "My Man and I," and "The Lonesome Road." They were a commercial success, among the first gospel music hits.

She appeared with the bandleader and entertainer Cab Calloway at the Cotton Club, Harlem's most famous nightclub. She performed at one of civil rights activist John Hammond's *From Spirituals to Swing* concerts on 23 December 1938.

She continued her career throughout the Second World War and recorded V discs (special recordings for the American military), one of the only gospel artists to do so.

In 1944, she recorded "Strange Things Happening Everyday," and for many, this was the very first rock 'n' roll recording. It reached Number Two on the Billboard

R&B (rhythm and blues) chart and greatly influenced future stars.

When Rosetta saw Marie Knight, a pianist and gospel singer, performing at a Mahalia Jackson concert, she was determined they should play together and invited her to go on tour. They recorded together, and it is widely believed they were in a relationship. In recent years, she has been celebrated as an LGBTQ+ icon.

Rosetta's popularity began to wane by the end of the 1940s. Marie was about to embark on a solo career but suffered a terrible tragedy when her children were killed in a house fire. The two women parted ways, although they would record together again.

In the 1950s, Rosetta continued to record and perform. She married again, this time at one of her concerts, in front of a crowd of 25,000 people, and found herself some backing singers whom she called her "Rosettes."

Her star rose again in 1964 when she was booked on a *Blues and Gospel Caravan* tour of Europe alongside Muddy Waters and Otis Spann, and she gained a new generation of fans. One concert, at a railway station in Manchester, was filmed for British television, and Eric Clapton, Brian Jones, and Keith Richards of the Rolling Stones were dazzled by her talent.

In 1970, she suffered a stroke and afterward had a leg amputated due to complications with diabetes. Still, she continued recording until her death on 9 October 1973; she had a session booked for the following day.

Little Richard named Rosetta as his greatest influence. Chuck Berry said his career had been "*one long Sister Rosetta Tharpe impersonation*" (She had even been the first to perform his famous "duck walk."). Bob Dylan called her "a powerful force of nature," and in his autobiography, Johnny Cash recalled being moved to tears at one of her concerts. As for Rosetta herself, she said, "*Can't no man play like me. My emotion is real, and my everyday life is filled with the same feeling. I've got Jesus in my heart.*"

24

IRENE MORGAN KIRKALDY -
STANDING FOR THE RIGHT TO SIT

When Irene Morgan awoke on 16 July 1944, she could never have imagined that her actions that day would see her imprisoned in jail, the subject of a benchmark court case that would eventually change society, and her being awarded the second highest honor of the president of the United States.

She was a young mother of two children, employed doing vital war work on the production line of an aircraft factory, but she had been staying with her mother in Gloucester, Virginia, to recuperate after suffering a miscarriage. That summer's day, she was returning home to Baltimore, Maryland, for an appointment with her doctor, hopeful she would soon be able to return to work.

She bought a ticket for the interstate Greyhound bus and sat next to another African-American woman holding a baby. There was not a segregated area for Black passengers; the rule was that they could not sit next to or face any white passengers.

During the journey, the driver stopped at Middlesex County, Virginia, and a white couple boarded. The driver told Irene and the woman with the baby to give up their seats and move. Irene refused. *"I had my ticket. I paid my fare, and I didn't think it was right for him to tell me that I would have to get up and give up my seat for another person who had just gotten on the bus,"* she recalled.

The driver took the bus to the next town. He went to get the sheriff, who boarded the bus and handed Irene an arrest warrant. She tore it into little pieces, threw them out of the window, and still would not move. The sheriff started to try and pull her to her feet, but she kicked him in his groin. *"He touched me; that's when I kicked him in a very bad place. He hobbled off, and another came on. I was going to bite him, but he looked dirty, so I clawed him instead; I ripped his shirt."* The second man threatened to hit her with his stick, and they were still arguing when the deputy sheriff arrived. Finally, she was removed and was taken to jail.

Irene was charged with resisting arrest and violating Virginia's Jim Crow transit law (the Jim Crow laws were state and local laws that had been introduced in the Southern states in the late 19th and early 20th centuries that enforced racial segregation). Her mother posted the $500 bail, and she was released.

On 18 October 1944, she arrived at a crowded courthouse with a Ku Klux Klan (a white supremacist, far-right terrorist organization) charter posted on the door to make her plea. She agreed to pay a $100 fine for resisting arrest but refused to accept the $10 fine for the segregation violation, which must have taken some courage in such a hostile, intimidating atmosphere.

Irene's case was taken up by the NAACP, and when the Supreme Court of Virginia ruled that she had broken the law, they appealed to the US Supreme Court. *"If something happens to you, which is wrong, the best thing to do is have it corrected in the best way you can. The best thing for me to do was to go to the Supreme Court,"* said Irene.

In 1946, she was represented by attorney William H. Hastie (who would be the first African American to be appointed as a federal district court judge), the former governor of the US Virgin Islands, and co-counsel Thurgood Marshall, a civil rights lawyer who, in 1967, became the first Black person to serve as a Supreme Court Justice.

They did not win Irene's case with the 14th Amendment to the Constitution, which forbade states to restrict the basic rights of citizens, but instead argued that segregation on interstate travel broke the Interstate Commerce Clause, and the jury agreed and ruled that it was unlawful.

Although the case and verdict were reported in the national media, it was quickly forgotten, and the ruling was often ignored in the Southern states; African Americans were removed from buses or arrested when they sat in seats deemed for white people. In 1947, activists from the Congress of Racial Equality made a stand and started a "Journey of Reconciliation," traveling on interstate buses, disregarding any segregation, and experiencing arrests and violent treatment, particularly in North Carolina.

Irene, the granddaughter of Virginia's enslaved people, continued to fight against oppression and prejudice. Although not a difficult or argumentative person, indeed, she is remembered by her family and friends for her kindness and humility. She would not accept segregation and campaigned for it to end, particularly in schools.

Her husband, Sherwood Morgan Sr., died in 1948, and she later married Stanley Kirkaldy. They moved to New York and opened a dry cleaning business and a child care center, but after Stanley had an accident and damaged his spine, leaving him quadriplegic, Irene devoted her life to caring for him while continuing to be a friend to people experiencing homelessness of New York—she invited them to her Thanksgiving dinner every year and let them do their laundry at her home.

In her sixties, Irene fulfilled a lifelong ambition and went to college. She graduated with a degree from St. John's University when she was 68, then completed a Master's Degree in Urban Studies at Queens College five years later.

It was in 2001 that President Bill Clinton awarded Irene with the Presidential Citizens Medal, which recognizes an individual "*who has performed exemplary deeds or services for his or her country or fellow citizens.*" The citation reads, "*When Irene Morgan boarded a bus for Baltimore in the summer of 1944, she took the first step on a journey that would change America forever... With courage and tenacity, she appealed her conviction and won a landmark Supreme Court victory that outlawed segregation in interstate transportation and helped make America a more just society."*

Irene died, aged ninety, in 2007. In a letter read at her funeral service held at Gloucester High School, Barack Obama (then a US Senator from Illinois) wrote how she had *"opened the doors of opportunity for people like me."*

Finally, from

1950 TO TODAY!

25

ROSA PARKS - ALABAMA ACTIVIST

"You must never be fearful about what you are doing when it is right."

One name that has become synonymous with the fight for civil rights in America in the 20th century is Rosa Parks, who challenged the prejudice, ignorance, and segregation being faced by American-African people every day in the Southern states of America with determination and dignity.

She was born in Pine Levels, Alabama, in 1913, but her parents separated when she was two, and her mother took her and her brother to live in Montgomery with her parents. Life was often frightening for a Black child in Alabama at that time; the Ku Klux Klan was a constant threat, burning African-American schools and churches and attacking and killing Black people.

Little Rosa was a sickly child who missed a lot of school due to chronic tonsillitis, and she often sat with her grandfather during the night as he sat with his rifle, ready to defend his home and family against these evil racists.

Rosa married Raymond Parks when she was nineteen, a barber and a lifelong member of the NAACP civil rights organization. He encouraged Rosa to complete her schooling, and then she started work as a seamstress. The Parks were popular and respected members of the large Black community of Montgomery. Rosa was secretary of the local NAACP branch and worked closely with E.D. Nixon, the president, a railway porter who was determined to challenge the Jim Crow laws that prevented Black children from receiving the same education opportunities (The schools for African Americans were inferior and overcrowded.), restricted Black people from using "white" libraries and even prohibited them from drinking from the water fountains that were reserved for white people.

On 1 December 1955, Rosa was returning home from work. Black people had to travel at the back of the buses with white people at the front; Rosa, many years earlier, had taken exception to the ridiculous rule that Black passengers, having paid their fare to the driver, had to then get off the bus and re-enter through the doors to the rear of the vehicle and had started to make her way through the front seats but had been grabbed by the driver, James Blake, who had shouted at her, telling her to use the rear door.

It was this same driver who, when the "white" seats were full, asked a row of Black passengers, including Rosa, to give up theirs and stand when more white people got on the bus.

Although the others got up, Rosa refused. *"People always say that I didn't give up my seat because I was tired, but that wasn't true. I was not tired physically... No, the only tired I was, was tired of giving in,"* she wrote in her autobiography.

Two police officers arrested Rosa and took her into custody, and on 5 December, she was found guilty of violating the segregation laws and given a suspended sentence and a $4 fine. The NAACP used her arrest and organized a large-scale boycott of the buses while she appealed her sentence that was managed by the newly formed Montgomery Improvement Association (MIA) with a young newcomer to the city, Dr. Martin Luther King, as its president.

This boycott inflamed the anger of the white supremacists in Alabama, and there were violent attacks; Dr. King and ED Nixon's homes were bombed, and Rosa received death threats, but the protest continued until, on 13 November 1956, the Supreme Court ruled that bus segregation was unconstitutional and illegal.

Of course, this ruling did not end racism in Alabama, but it was now clear that African Americans were not prepared to passively accept unfair and unjust laws, and Rosa was regarded as the "mother of the civil rights movement" that had turned the tide.

She continued to fight for civil rights throughout her life, and when she died in 2005, she was the first woman and second African American to lay in state in the Rotunda of the US Capitol.

"I would like to be remembered as a person who wanted to be free... so other people would also be free," she said.

26

DR. MARTIN LUTHER KING JR - BIG DREAMS

"I have a dream that one day this nation will rise up and live out the true meaning of its creed: that all men are created equal."

On 28 August 1963, a speech that changed America and much of the Western world was delivered at the Lincoln Memorial in Washington, DC. Almost a quarter of a million people, Black and white, had gathered in the capital for the March on Washington for Jobs and Freedom, and Dr. King was the final speaker.

He spoke for seventeen minutes about his vision for America, a land of racial equality and freedom for everybody, and the country's failure to keep the promises to the descendants of enslaved people a hundred years (or so) after President Abraham Lincoln had signed the Emancipation Declaration.

With drama and tension, Dr. King combined his own thoughts with words from the scriptures and echoes from other preachers. It is considered among the finest speeches in the English language and stirred the souls of so many because, it is said, it was given "by the right man, with the right words, to the right audience at the right time."

Martin Luther King was born in Atlanta, Georgia in 1929. He attended segregated schools and then studied at Morehouse College, followed by Crozer Theological Seminary in Pennsylvania, where he was elected president of his mostly white senior class. He enrolled at Boston University in 1951 and was awarded his doctorate four years later.

He became the pastor of Dexter Avenue Baptist Church in Montgomery, Alabama, and a prominent figure in the civil rights struggles there. After leading the Montgomery bus boycott in support of Rosa Parks, he became president of the Southern Christian Leadership Conference, a new organization inspired by Mahatma Gandhi's nonviolent resistance against Colonial Britain in India earlier that century.

Between 1957 and 1968, he addressed thousands of protests, civil rights meetings, and African-American organizations, traveling some six million miles. In 1963, his peaceful protest led to confrontations between Black students and the white civic authorities in Birmingham, Alabama, one of the most racially segregated cities in the country. A peaceful walk from the 16th Street Baptist Church to the Mayor's office in City Hall to request an end to segregation saw over a thousand protesters arrested and others, including children, targeted with high-pressure water hoses and attack dogs.

The eyes of the world could finally see the reality of the situation for African Americans in the Southern states. Dr. King, one of those arrested, wrote an open "Letter from Birmingham City Jail," calling for people to break unjust laws as their moral responsibility. *"Injustice anywhere is a threat to justice everywhere,"* he wrote.

The following year, he was awarded the Nobel Peace Prize. In his acceptance speech in Norway, he said, "I believe that unarmed truth and unconditional love will have the final word in reality. This is why right temporarily defeated is stronger than evil triumphant," and donated the prize money of $54,123 to the civil rights movement. That same year, the Civil Rights Act was passed.

Dr. King had received death threats since the early 1950s and had survived a vicious knife attack in 1958. He was always aware his life could end in an assassination. He spoke of it often and told his supporters that his death could not stop the fight for civil rights.

In February 1968, he traveled to Memphis, Tennessee, where Black sanitation workers were protesting against unequal pay and poor conditions—white workers were paid more and had uniforms, restrooms, unions, and employment rights—which they did not. When two Black workers were killed during their work, they began a strike, and Dr. King joined them in a protest march.

Despite being delayed by a bomb threat, he arrived at the Mason Temple (the world headquarters of the Church of God in Christ) on 3 April and delivered his famous "I've Been to the Mountaintop" speech. The following day, he leaned over his motel room balcony to speak to the Reverend Jesse Jackson on the neighboring balcony when he was shot by James Earl Ray from a house opposite.

It is not certain what Ray's motives were. Dr. King was planning a large-scale protest against poverty in Washington and had started to speak out against the Vietnam War, so many believed it had been organized by his enemies.

Dr. King and his legacy of hope and healing will forever be remembered in America and the wider world. His dream and his powerful, impactful words are as relevant and thought-provoking today as they were fifty years ago.

27

MUHAMMAD ALI - "THE GREATEST"

On 28 April 1967, a handsome, confident, and articulate twenty-five-year-old Black man from Louisville, Kentucky, formally refused to be inducted into the US Army, then fighting a war against Vietnam.

Between 1964 and 1973, the US military drafted 2.2 million young men to fight in that war, and this young man was the World Heavyweight Boxing Champion, Muhammad Ali. After completing his physical examination, he would not step forward when his name was called at the induction ceremony.

Two months later, he was convicted of draft evasion and was sentenced to five years in prison, a fine of $10,000, and was banned from boxing for three years. He was also stripped of his heavyweight title.

Born Cassius Marcellus Clay on 14 January 1942, Muhammad had shown great promise as a boxer from an early age. He won a gold medal at the 1960 Olympic

Games in Rome, and then after becoming professional, he battled to become the heavyweight champion in a fight against Sonny Liston on 25 February 1964.

That same year, Muhammad converted to Islam and rejected his birth name, calling it his "slave name." His religious beliefs were the reason for his conscientious objection to fighting in the Vietnam War, and this would have been considered a justifiable reason for refusing the draft, but he had acknowledged that he would fight in an Islamic Holy War, if he were asked. When he was asked to explain why he would not join up, he said, "*Why should they as me to put on a uniform and go 10,000 miles from home and drop bombs and bullets on brown people in Vietnam while so-called Negro people in Louisville are treated like dogs?*"

Muhammad was given the harshest sentence possible for his refusal because the American public was beginning to turn against the Vietnam War. A hundred US Army soldiers were dying every day, and the financial costs to the country were astronomical. Muhammad vowed to fight against his conviction so he didn't go to prison but remained free, on bail, while his appeal was being processed. Despite newspaper campaigns to damage his reputation, the world began to listen to him and see him as more than an athlete. A great many people grew sympathetic to his cause.

The Supreme Court overturned his conviction in 1971, and Muhammad was able to return to boxing. He would win the heavyweight championship three times, and many boxing enthusiasts believe he was simply "the greatest." He was almost certainly the fastest. He shuffled his feet back and forth throughout his fights as though he was dancing.

After a long career in which he lost and regained his title, he retired in 1981, and after a long battle with Parkinson's disease, he died in 2016. He never regretted his stance against the war; *"Some people thought I was a hero. Some people said what I did was wrong. But everything I did was according to my conscience. I wasn't trying to be a leader. I just wanted to be free. And I made a stand all people, not just Black people, should have thought about making..."* he said. Today, he is remembered as much for his activism and philanthropy as for his undoubted skills in the boxing ring.

28

NELSON MANDELA - "IT ALWAYS SEEMS IMPOSSIBLE UNTIL IT'S DONE."

Between 1948 and 1994, the people of South Africa were divided by an appalling policy called Apartheid (the word for "separateness" or "being apart" in Afrikaans). The all-white government introduced and enforced a regime by which Black people were kept apart from white people. It was racism by law, supported by the courts.

Black people were forced to live in particular areas without proper schools, hospitals, or services. They were kept very poor, and thousands of children ended up working in factories or laboring on farms to help their families survive and had barely any education. Any contact between Black and white people was limited. Black people were not allowed to go to the beach or use public toilets, and interracial marriages were illegal. Although there were some white South Africans who opposed Apartheid, Black people were not allowed to vote, so these rules were unlikely to change.

Despite being exhausted from overwork, demoralized from the cruel treatment of the ruling government, and suppressed by the ruling classes, Black activists were not going to accept this treatment and fought against Apartheid. One of these crusaders was Nelson Rolihlahla Mandela.

Madiba (a name derived from his Xhosa clan meaning "father," which Black South Africans call him as a title of respect) was born in 1918 in Mvezo, South Africa. After attending a segregated school, he won a place at the University of Fort Hare, which was then the country's only university for Black students, to study law. It was there that he began to seriously oppose the government and Apartheid. This opposition led to his expulsion from the university, and he moved to the township of Soweto to complete his studies. There, he joined the African National Congress (ANC), a campaign group for Black South Africans' civil rights.

At first, the ANC used nonviolent methods to resist Apartheid, such as demonstrations and strikes, but these peaceful protests had little impact, so in June 1952, Madiba led the Defiance Campaign, a new drive that encouraged Black people to break the unjust laws they were expected to abide by. The South African authorities came down heavily on the lawbreakers, and more than 8,000 people, including Madiba, were jailed for offenses, such as violating curfews and refusing to carry identification passes.

This campaign forced the ANC into the spotlight and not just in South Africa. After his release from jail, Madiba continued his fight. He was arrested again in 1956 on treason charges but acquitted. He had started to believe the ANC's peaceful policy was never going to work, and with this in mind, he traveled to Algeria to learn sabotage techniques and guerrilla warfare.

As soon as he returned to South Africa, he was arrested for traveling without a permit, and when the authorities discovered why he had left the country, he and his colleagues were charged with sabotage. Madiba felt sure they would be found guilty and executed, so he used his Rivonia Trial (as it has become known) to campaign against Apartheid and publicize the brutality of the regime. He gave a four-hour speech defending his actions. *"It is a struggle for the right to live... if it needs be, it is an ideal for which I am prepared to die,"* he said.

Madiba was sentenced to life imprisonment, with just a half-hour prison visit each year. The conditions were very harsh, and the inmates were forced to work in a limestone quarry. He remained there for twenty-seven years and became the world's most famous prisoner.

Countries of the United Nations began to question his imprisonment and his (and others') opposition to Apartheid, a regime that was clearly out of step with the rest of the world, and called for sanctions to be made against South Africa. Students and young people were particularly vocal about what they saw as an atrocity. By the 1980s, international disapproval had grown to such an extent that the country's new president, FW de Klerk, was forced to start dismantling Apartheid. On 11 February 1990, he released Madiba from prison.

The world watched as the slight, aged figure walked out of the front gate of the Victor Verster Prison in the suburbs of Cape Town and then raised his fist in triumph.

Despite his advanced years (he was seventy-one) and the years of captivity that must have had an impact on his mental health, Madiba worked with the president to establish a new, fairer constitution for South Africa, and in 1991, Apartheid formally ended. The two men shared the Nobel Peace Prize for this outstanding achievement.

Nelson Mandela, as head of the ANC, was elected president in the free and peaceful elections of 1994. He served for five years, and he founded the Truth and Reconciliation Commission to help people affected by the years of segregation, both for Black and white, to come to terms with their experiences.

After leaving office in 1999, Madiba spent his final years campaigning to end poverty and raise AIDS awareness—a major public health issue in South Africa. He died in 2013, aged ninety-five.

This extraordinary man inspired a generation and, through his fight to eliminate discrimination and segregation in his country, became a living symbol of hope and empowerment. "*It is in your hands to make a better world for all who live in it*," he said.

29

SERENA WILLIAMS - MOMMA SMASH

Few athletes have demonstrated such sporting excellence as Serena Williams, simply the greatest female tennis player of all time.

Serena was born in Compton, California, on 26 September 1981. Her father, Richard Williams, had taken tennis lessons and was determined that Serena and Venus, her older sister, should be tennis professionals. He made an extensive plan (of 85 pages) to this end. His girls started playing on public tennis courts when Serena was only four and a half years old.

Richard was a first-class but tough and demanding coach. He had a difficult childhood blighted by racism, and he wanted the very best for his daughters. He spent long hours with them, developing their strength and perfecting their game. Then, in 1991, the family moved to Florida so Serena and Venus could attend a tennis academy there.

To begin with, Venus, taller than the two girls, had the advantage, but Serena built her powerful frame and developed a mental attitude that just would not accept defeat. She learned to attack and scrap for every point, and this, with her unshakable belief in herself, made it incredibly difficult for any opponent that faced her on the tennis court.

In 1999, aged seventeen, Serena broke through and won the US Open. For a year or so, Venus won four of six grand slam titles, but then Serena came into her own with her smooth but deadly serve and attacking style of play. And the Williams sisters, as doubles partners, were outstanding. Several of their defeated opponents remarked that it was almost as if they were playing a different game.

Between 2002 and 2003, Serena dominated women's tennis. She won four grand slams in a row to achieve what has become known as her "Serena Slam" and seemed unbeatable. Other players on the circuit had no option but to adapt to her play style to keep up.

In 2003, however, everything changed. After recovering from knee surgery, the tragic killing of Serena and Venus's oldest half-sister, Yetunde, in a drive-by shooting deeply affected them and the Williams family. Serena suffered from a breakdown followed by a long period of depression; it wasn't until 2007 that she was well enough to be able to return to tennis and her winning form. She made an astonishing comeback and won the Australian Open.

Serena and her sister had a huge impact on helping Black and people of color to both play tennis and support the game. Before their dominance, only Evonne Goolagong and Zina Garrison had been the only Black women to reach grand slam finals in the Open era, but the traditionally conservative game has now had a renaissance, with several Black female athletes reaching grand slam finals.

Now she has retired from tennis after a long career that has spanned three decades, Serena has her own family and has proved to be a formidable businesswoman with a particular flair for the fashion and accessories industries. She speaks fluent French and was the first Black female athlete to be photographed on the cover of Vogue magazine. She is also a passionate advocate for gender, positive body image, and racial equality.

She understands the importance of being an inspiration for young women and breaking barriers. "There weren't a lot of role models for me to look up to and say, 'Wow, I want to look like this!' I kind of had to be that role and be that person… Venus and I started out being successful, continued to be successful, and we were unapologetically ourselves. We were not afraid to wear braids. We weren't afraid to be Black in tennis. And that was different," she said.

30

OPRAH WINFREY - LADY O

Oprah Winfrey is one of American television's most recognized and enduring faces. As well as hosting the award-winning Oprah Winfrey Show for twenty-five years (1986–2011), she is a producer, an actress, and a philanthropist. She has founded her own cable network, a lifestyle magazine (*O, The Oprah Magazine*), and a film company (Harpo).

She was born on 29 January 1954 at a farm in Kosciusko, Mississippi. Her parents separated soon afterward, and little Oprah was brought up by her maternal grandmother. They moved to a suburb in Milwaukee when she was six. There was no money, and life was very hard.

When she was twelve, she went to live with her father in Nashville, Tennessee, for a time, then back to Milwaukee, then backward and forward to stay with each of her parents throughout her teens.

Although this must have been unsettling, she has said that it was her father's firm belief in the importance of education that made her fulfill her potential. After leaving school, she won a full scholarship to Tennessee State University.

After graduating at just nineteen years old, she landed her first television job at a CBS station in Nashville, reporting the news. The following year, she left to present a new morning talk show that was an immediate success; her skilled but warm and informal interview style made her show compulsive viewing in many American households.

In 1984, The Oprah Winfrey Show was launched in Chicago and soon topped the ratings. Two years later, still going from strength to strength, it was lengthened from thirty minutes to an hour-long show.

In that same year, Oprah starred in Steven Spielberg's acclaimed film, *The Color Purple*, an adaptation of the classic Alice Walker novel. Audiences and critics were moved by her sensitive performance, and she was nominated for an Academy Award.

From lessons she has learned from her own experiences and career, Oprah has been committed to helping people, especially women and girls, escape poverty and oppression through education and opportunity. She suffered sexual and physical abuse growing up, and this has made her determined to work toward safeguarding young people. Her campaign for a national database of child abusers, known as "Oprah's Bill," became a part of the US National Child Protection Act in 1993.

She has donated a great deal of money to causes dear to her heart, including $400 million to fund higher education projects and programs, to enable schools to help girls in South Africa. During the COVID-19 pandemic, she committed $12 million to vulnerable and poverty-stricken communities where she had lived.

Oprah is one of the richest and most influential women in America. Her ability to connect with people, her honesty about her own difficulties, and that she has never forgotten her roots have made her enduringly popular. She is a great communicator who has completely changed television talk shows, always encouraging positivity and self-belief.

31

MICHAEL JORDAN - A BULL AND THE GOAT

 "I can accept failure, everyone fails at something. But I can't accept not trying."

- Michael Jordan

Michael Jordan is often considered to be the greatest basketball player of all time. He won six championships, five MVPs (Most Valuable Player), and ten scoring titles in his long career.

MJ was born in New York on 17 February 1963 and grew up in Wilmington, North Carolina. He was gifted at sports as a boy, and once it was clear how tall he would be, basketball was the obvious choice; fully grown, he would stand at 6 feet and 6 inches (1.98 meters). At the University of North Carolina at Chapel Hill, he made the winning basket against Georgetown in the 1982 national championship game and was named "player of the year."

His team won gold medals for the United States at the 1984 Olympic Games in Los Angeles and the 1992 Games in Barcelona. He played for thirteen seasons with the Chicago Bulls (1984–1993, then 1995–1995) but came out of retirement, aged thirty-eight, to play for the Washington Wizards for two seasons, just "*for the love of the game.*" MJ still has the record for the most scoring titles in National Basketball Association (NBA) history.

MJ is known for his superb athleticism. His amazing, almost superhuman leaps have earned him the nickname "Air Jordan" or "His Airness." Basketball fans were thrilled and amazed by his expert shooting and gritty defense play, but his mindset has set him apart from other players. He used visualization techniques to imagine himself taking the winning shots well before the game began. This strong mental conviction has been of great benefit to players of other sports and at other levels who have learned his techniques.

Since retiring, MJ has earned millions from endorsements (his Nike "Air Jordan" basketball shoes are enduringly popular) and smart investments. He has also donated $10 million to Make-A-Wish, a charitable organization that grants wonderful and unique experiences for children with life-threatening illnesses. He has personally granted more than a hundred "wishes," and as he is still one of America's most popular sportsmen, he is still one of the most requested "wishes."

In 2021, through his Jordan Brand company, he pledged $100 million to combat some issues that Black communities have fought against. In the months that followed a series of high-profile killings of Black people in police custody, the world was shocked with a stark and graphic insight into violence faced by some African-American people by those in authority, MJ wanted to play his part. He has provided grants for Black ex-offenders and their families and the Black Votes Matter organization.

32

TIGER WOODS - CHILD STAR

The first time the world saw Tiger Woods swinging his golf club, he was just two years old. The talented toddler was featured on The Mike Douglas television show in 1978. The following year, the child prodigy had shot 48 over nine holes—before he had even started elementary school.

TIGER WAS BORN IN CYPRESS, California, on 30 December 1975. His father was of African-American, Native American, and Asian descent, and his mother was Thai. He was named Eldrick Tont Woods, but from the start, his father called him "Tiger," and the name just stuck! Rather than labeling himself as Black, Tiger prefers to acknowledge his full heritage and calls himself "Cablinasian"—Caucasian, Black, Native American, and Asian ancestry.

.   .   .

AFTER ATTENDING STANFORD UNIVERSITY, Tiger turned professional in 1996 and has had an astonishing career. In 2091, he was the first player of African-American or Asian descent to win the Masters, the first major golf tournament of the year held at Augusta National Golf Club in Georgia, and the first player to consecutively win all four of the major golf tournaments—the Masters, the US Open, the British Open, and the Professional Golfers' Association (PGA) Championship.

HE HAS BEEN RECOGNIZED as one of the greatest golfers of all time and one of the most famous athletes in modern times. He is highly intelligent and has an exceptional memory. He credits his father with his mental strength. The Vietnam veteran would encourage Tiger to take the same shot again and again, whatever the distraction.

TIGER'S particular talent is for ball striking, and he has improved his performance by learning cognitive skills and working on his perception, decision-making, and reaction time. He has suffered serious leg, ankle, and back injuries that needed surgery and forced him to step back from golfing. He then had a serious car accident, and almost immediately afterward, problems in his personal life became public. But Tiger had not finished with golf, and in 2018, he made a remarkable comeback.

· · ·

No LONGER SUCH a young man and facing competition from new, exciting players, Tiger is still a force to be reckoned with. In 2023, after further surgery, "*I'm playing really well. I'm hitting the ball great. My putting's good…*," he said as he prepared for yet another return to the top.

33

PELÉ PÉROLA NEGRA (THE BLACK PEARL)

The Brazilian player, according to Fédération Internationale de Football Association (FIFA), "the greatest" and known to fans as the "God of Football," was the most famous and highly paid footballer in the world for many years. He was also the mainstay of Brazil's legendary national football team that won the World Cup in 1958, 1962, and 1970.

FOOTBALL HAS HAD a massive following throughout the world in modern times, particularly in South America and Europe. It is characterized by passionate support, and while Pelé was playing, Brazil became the heart and soul of the "beautiful game." Spectators, professional players, and school kids watched him score goal after goal, with his almost telepathic ability to anticipate his teammates and the opposition players moves.

. . .

PELÉ WAS born Edson Arantes do Nascimento on 23 November 1940 in Três Corações, Brazil. His father was a footballer, and young Pelé grew up in poverty in Bauru in São Paulo. Unable to afford a football, he and his brothers learned their skills on socks stuffed full of newspaper and then tied with string or large grapefruits. He played for several teams as a boy and, aged fifteen, signed a professional contract with Santos FC.

FROM THE START, the club knew they had a star. Pelé was the top scorer in the league that season, and within ten months, he was selected to play for his country's national team. As soon as

European clubs saw his mesmerizing talent in the 1958 World Cup, they began to offer huge sums of money to sign him, but the Brazilian government quickly realized how valuable he was to his country and declared him a national treasure. Pelé was not for sale.

PELÉ SCORED his *gol de placa* (goal worthy of a plaque) against Fluminense FC at the Maracaña (football stadium in Rio de Janeiro) in March 1961, and a memorial to that sporting achievement was commissioned and dedicated to "the most beautiful goal in the history of the Maracaña."

EVERYONE WANTED TO WATCH HIM. In 1967, he traveled to Nigeria with his team, Santos. The country was in a civil war, but a 48-hour ceasefire was agreed so Pelé could play there.

ON 19 NOVEMBER 1969, in his 909th match, he scored his 1,000th goal. He retired in 1974 but soon made a comeback and signed a $7 million contract with the New York Cosmos in the North American Soccer League to promote his beloved football in the United States.

THROUGHOUT HIS CAREER AND RETIREMENT, Pelé was showered with honors and awards. In 1978, he was awarded the International Peace Award. In 1980, he was awarded Athlete of the Century by the French magazine L'Equipe. In 1999, he received that same title from the International Olympic Committee and an honorary knighthood from Queen Elizabeth II at a ceremony at Buckingham Palace in 1997.

IN 1995, the Brazilian president appointed Pelé Minister of Sport in a bid to try and rid the game of corruption, but it was a thankless task.

AWAY FROM FOOTBALL, he dedicated his life to causes that mattered to him: sport, ecology and the environment, and fighting against poverty. He was an ambassador for several charities and, in 2918, launched the Pelé

Foundation to help impoverished and deprived children worldwide.

PELÉ DIED of cancer on 29 December 2022 at the age of 82. Brazil mourned their greatest star over three days, and thousands of people, many wearing the Brazilian team's yellow and green No. 10 jerseys or the black and white Santos shirts he had worn. At the time of his death, he was still the joint-top goal scorer for Brazil, with 77 goals in 92 games.

ON 26 APRIL 2023, the word *"Pelé"* was added to the Brazilian Portuguese dictionary. Its meaning? "Exceptional, incomparable, unique."

34

SEAN COMBS - "THE SAGA CONTINUES..."

Sean Combs, also known by his stage names "Puff Daddy," "Puffy," "P. Diddy," and "Diddy," was born in Harlem, New York, on 4 November 1969. His father was murdered when Sean was just two years old, and in 1974, his mother moved to Mt. Vernon.

Sean attended a Catholic boys' school in the Bronx. It is there, it is said, that he was given the nickname "Puffy" by his classmates, who noticed the way he would puff out his chest to make himself seem bigger on the sports field.

After leaving school, he was accepted at Howard University to study business and administration, but when he started an internship at Uptown Records, he knew he had found his vocation and left the university for a career in music.

He quickly made a name for himself at Uptown; he understood the industry and its consumers and had a natural and instinctive flair for marketing their recording artists just the right way. In 1987, when he was just nine-teen, Sean was promoted to vice president of A & R at Uptown and launched the careers of several stars, notably Mary J. Blige.

It was not all a success, however. In 1991, tragedy struck at a hip-hop celebrity charity basketball game that Sean was promoting at City College, New York; nine people were crushed to death, and another twenty-one were injured when crowds pushed their way inside. The game had been organized to benefit AIDS education after the basketball superstar Magic Johnson had spoken of his HIV status. *"What happened at City College is the worst thing that ever happened to me,"* he said, *"I felt such a form of sorrow and remorse..."*

He was fired from Uptown in 1993 and launched his own venture, Bad Boy Entertainment, with Arista Records. He wanted to make hip-hop records and struck gold when he signed with the Notorious B.I.G. and even contributed his own voice to the artist's smash hit, *Mo Money Mo Problems.*

In 1997, the Notorious B.I.G was killed in a drive-by shooting. Later that same year, Sean released the first of his own albums as a hip-hop artist, *No Way Out*, and his single, *I'll Be Missing You*—with the melody from The Police's Every Breath You Take—as a tribute to his fallen friend. It was a huge success and won him a Grammy award.

In a bid to move on from the traumatic sadnesses he had experienced, Sean moved on from his Puff Daddy stage name and began to use "P. Diddy" instead (he dropped the

"P" in 2001 and so became known as "Diddy"). He also performed on Broadway in a revival of Lorraine Hansberry's play, *A Raisin in the Sun.*

Two years later, Sean ventured into film and acted in *Made*, and then—to critical acclaim—played a murderer facing the electric chair in *Monster's Ball* (2001). He also ventured into television and produced a competitive reality series, *Making the Band.*

In 2013, he launched Revolt TV, a television network focused on news and modern culture aimed at an African-American audience.

Sean's ability to take on anything, with his clear, focused ambition, has built him a formidable business empire. He has launched a clothing brand and has worked with companies to endorse their products. In December 2017, he formed a syndicate of African-American athletes and bought the National Football League's Carolina Panthers. His "Daddy's House Social Program" was founded to help underprivileged children reach their potential, particularly in urban areas, and he continues to be an award-winning recording artist and producer.

As well as amassing a huge amount of money (estimated to be in the region of $500 million), he has become an extremely influential voice in the entertainment industry and an inspirational figure for young people—especially those with a love for hip-hop.

35

BARACK OBAMA - A NEW BIRTH OF FREEDOM

On 20 January 2009, Barack Obama took the oath of office in a ceremony at the West Front of the US Capitol and became the 44th president of the United States of America. The world watched as the son of a Black father from Kenya and a white mother from Kansas was sworn in, his hand on the Bible used by President Abraham Lincoln at his first inauguration, and his African-American wife, Michelle, at his side.

Crowds of people amassed outside the building; according to official estimates, there were approximately 1.8 million people there. When the new president addressed them, he spoke of the challenges he faced: the worsening economic crisis, unaffordable healthcare, failing schools, and the war against terrorism and radical-ization. But he also said, *"A man whose father less than sixty years ago might not have been served at a local restaurant can now stand before you to take a most sacred oath."*

Barack Hussain Obama II was born on 4 August 1961 in Honolulu, Hawaii. After graduating from Harvard University in 1988, where he was the first African-American President of the Harvard Law Review, he joined a small law firm that specialized in civil rights cases, where a young Michelle Robinson was assigned to be his mentor.

Michelle and Barack were married in 1992, and they have two daughters.

In 1996, Barack launched his first campaign for political office and was elected to the Illinois Senate, and in 2004, he was elected to the US Senate. He gave an address at the Democratic Convention that same year that impressed his peers; many earmarked him as a future president, but they had no idea it would happen so quickly. Just four years later, he was the Democratic Party's preferred presidential candidate and defeated the Republican nominee, Senator John McCain of Arizona, to take office in the White House.

During his two terms as president, Barack passed healthcare reform. The Affordable Care Act enabled more than twenty million Americans to buy health insurance, many of whom, with pre-existing conditions, had been refused coverage until this reform.

When he had taken office, the economy had slumped. Barack invested $831 billion and introduced policies to aid his country's recovery, modernize infrastructure, expand educational opportunities, and fund research projects while ensuring the poorest in society were protected.

He ended US combat missions in Iraq and Afghanistan and, in 2011, authorized the US special forces raid in Pakistan that killed the al-Qaeda leader, Osama bin Laden, the deadly enemy of the United States and responsible for the 9/11 attacks on the World Trade Center and the Pentagon.

He also used his office to educate the public about the serious dangers of climate change and, through diplomacy and promises of investment, secured a global agreement with 195 nations to combat pollution.

In 2009, Barack Obama was the fourth president of the United States to be awarded the Nobel Peace Prize for his "extraordinary efforts to strengthen international diplomacy and cooperation between peoples."

After serving his two terms, Barack left office on 20 January 2017. He has remained in Washington, DC, and has continued to actively support the Democratic Party. He and Michelle are still involved in campaigning for civil rights, have both written books, and have produced documentaries. Barack has long been commended as a great speaker and has turned his skills to narrating and won an Emmy for his work on "Our National Parks," a Netflix documentary series.

It isn't easy to decide exactly what Barack's legacy will be. He will always be remembered as America's first African-American president, but he was determined to be so much more than that. When his presidency ended, the Democratic candidate Donald J. Trump succeeded him, so many of Barack's reforms and achievements were abandoned or overturned, including his Affordable Care Act (known as "Obamacare") and the Paris climate change agreement. He and Michelle have remained popular with the public and highly respected and inspirational on the international stage, where their voices are still listened to.

36

KANYE WEST - A FLAWED GENIUS

Kanye West is one of the most controversial celebrities of his age, and he has learned to use and even celebrate public debate over his words and deeds.

He was born in Atlanta, Georgia in 1977. His father, Ray, is an award-winning photojournalist and, more recently, a pastor, and his mother a professor of English at Chicago University. They separated when Kanye was very young, and he moved to South Side Chicago with his mother. When he was ten, they spent a year in China as part of an exchange program organized by the university.

When he returned to Chicago, he began to take an interest in the local hip-hop scene. After school, he started studying at university but soon realized it wasn't for him, and he found work in the music business. He had a natural talent for producing hip-hop and was soon the first choice for many up-and-coming artists, but he wanted to make his own music.

He found it difficult to persuade record companies that he had something to say as a hip-hop artist since he came from a middle-class background. This genre was closely associated with poor, disadvantaged young people at the time.

Kanye persevered with his dream. On 23 October 2002, after working late in a California studio, he was driving home and fell asleep at the wheel. His car crashed into oncoming traffic, and he was left with a serious injury to his jaw; to heal it, his doctor had to wire his mouth closed and told him to rest.

But Kanye had other ideas. *"The accident gave me the opportunity to do what I really wanted to do. During that recovery period, I just spent all my time honing my craft and making 'The College Dropout,'"* he said.

When it was released, this album was a massive success and made worldwide sales of more than 4 million copies. It was acclaimed for its politically aware, insightful, and humorous lyrics. It included the track *"Through the Wire,"* which he rapped just three days after his accident.

This was to be the start of a hugely influential recording career. It has been said that Kanye has changed the direction of hip-hop, particularly with the content of his music; he has rapped about religion, his faith, and other personal issues, constantly experimenting and adapting his style.

He is not afraid to speak out. After Hurricane Katrina devastated New Orleans in 2005, he criticized the government's slow response to provide aid for the stricken citizens, saying that the president, George W. Bush, "*doesn't care about Black people,*" words that resonated among all communities. President Bush later said it was one of the worst moments of his term in office.

In 2012, Kanye started dating the reality star and entrepreneur Kim Kardashian, and despite the public questioning whether it was a publicity stunt, they married in 2014 and had a family. Kanye has always had a strong interest in fashion, image, and street style. In 2015, he teamed up with Adidas to launch a range of clothing and sneakers under the brand name YEEZY. With Kanye's popularity and clever marketing, they sold out in minutes. He has released several fashion collections on his YEEZY label and has released collections at New York Fashion Week.

Kanye's personal life came under strain, particularly after he announced his support for Donald J. Trump and began considering a political career. In 2018, he defended a comment suggesting African-American people had coop-erated in their enslavement in earlier times. He announced that he suffered from mental health issues, particularly bipolar, and explored this condition in his 2018 album *Ye*.

In 2022, Kanye hit the headlines again. At Paris Fashion Week, his models wore "White Lives Matter" T-shirts on the runway. He explained, "*I saw white people wearing shirts that said 'Black Lives Matter' like they were doing me a favor by having a T-shirt that reminded me that my life mattered, like I didn't already know that."*

In the same year, however, he made a series of anti-Semitic (anti-Jewish) comments on social media that were widely condemned and resulted in him being locked out of his Instagram and Twitter accounts and an end to his collaboration with Adidas.

With 24 Grammy awards (and 75 nominations), more than any other rap artist, and having sold more than 160 million records, Kanye's dedication, hard work, and desire to push forward have given him wealth and influence. By breaking the stereotype that rappers are concerned only with crime, drugs, and money, he changed the appeal of hip-hop to a much wider and more diverse audience.

37

SANTAN DAVE - RAPPING FOR REFORM

David Orobosa Omoregie was born on 5 January 1998. His parents were Nigerian, his mother a nurse and his father a pastor. He had two older brothers, Christopher and Benjamin, and the family lived in the Angell Town area of Brixton, South London.

When Dave was just four months old, his father was deported to Nigeria. He had not realized his visa was temporary, fearing they would be in danger there; his mother, Juliet Doris, fled with her three boys. For a long while, they were homeless and slept on South London buses until, eventually, when Dave was seven, they found a home in Streatham, South London.

Dave began composing as a young boy; he watched his older brothers practicing rapping, and when he was fourteen, he taught himself to play the electric keyboard, a Christmas gift from his mother.

It was a difficult childhood in many ways. Both of Dave's brothers were in trouble with the law. Christopher was involved in the gang murder of Sofyen Belamouadden at London Victoria Station in March 2010 and was imprisoned for life. In 2014, Benjamin was found guilty of robbery charges and imprisoned for four years. Dave saw the traumatic impact this had on his mother.

Juliette Doris worked long hours, hoping to keep her youngest son away from crime. He was a serious, thoughtful boy. After leaving St. Mark's Academy in Mitcham, he studied law, philosophy with ethics, politics, and sound design at Richmond upon Thames College in Twickenham but decided not to go to university; he wanted a career in music.

He started by performing online, particularly on Black Box, a YouTube channel for freestyle rap, and soon gained attention. His first album, "Psychodrama," was inspired by therapy his brother Christopher was undergoing in prison—in which offenders role-play their experiences to help them understand the consequences of their crimes and how they came to break the law.

The album was a bestseller, and Dave received the Music of Black Origin (MOBO) Best Newcomer award. He dedicated much of his success to Christopher and spoke about the need for prison reform; his brother's voice, in a telephone conversation with Dave from prison, was featured in one of the tracks, and this has brought about strong disapproval, particularly from those who knew and loved Sofyen Belamouadden.

While he has said that he understands the need for punishment, Dave explained, "*Prison hosts a lot of normal people, a lot of family men who were caught in a tight situation or a dark place. I don't think that one moment in people's life should define them.*" He knew Jack Merritt, the London Terror Attack victim who was working on a rehabilitation program for offenders developed by Cambridge University, which had helped Dave's brother. After Jack's murder by the recently released terrorist Usman Khan, he called him his "brother in arms."

With his next album, he continued to explore uncomfortable issues, such as domestic violence, knife crime, and immigration. His track Heart Attack is a particularly moving piece that begins with a reporter's voice talking about street violence and ends with his mother's voice, emotionally recalling her journey to the United Kingdom.

Dave was awarded an Ivor Novello Award in 2018 for the track "Question Time," which explored issues, such as Syria and the British Government's lackluster response to the Grenfell fire and, in 2022, a BRIT award for Best Hip-Hop/Grime/Rap Act. But it was at the 2020 BRIT award ceremony that his voice was first heard by many; he performed his hit song "Black"—a rap that celebrates the diverse Black culture and addresses the ways that racism is still a major problem in Britain but added an extra verse in which he laid out a series of examples of discrimination and racial abuse—from the Windrush scandal to the British press's treatment of Meghan Markle.

Although, the following day, government ministers were quick to deny any racism, representatives for Black community groups said his words had clearly resonated with people.

38

KOBE BRYANT - A MAMBA MEMORIAL

While Kobe Bryant watched Quentin Tarantino's 2003 film *Kill Bill*, he really liked the name of a lethal assassin, "Black Mamba," and decided to use it for his alter ego. On the basketball court, he was no longer charming, quietly spoken Kobe Bryant, and he was the fiercely competitive, single-minded athlete who would never give up. And, as he said, "*I always aim to kill the opposition,*" just like Africa's deadliest snake.

Born on 23 August 1978 in Philadelphia, Pennsylvania, Kobe's talent and love for basketball was clear from his school days. Rather than studying at university, he went straight to the National Basketball Association (NBA) and played for the Los Angeles Lakers throughout his twenty-year career.

With the Lakers, he won five NBA championships and two Olympic gold medals, and when he retired in 2016, he was the NBA's third-highest all-time scorer.

He believed his phenomenal success was due to his mental attitude, and he called this his "Mamba mentality," an outlook not just for athletes, with five "pillars": passion, obsession, relentlessness, resilience, and fearlessness. He founded the Mamba Sports Academy, with a particular focus on promoting women's basketball, with this in mind. *"Hard work outweighs talent every time,"* he said.

In 2003, Kobe faced a sexual assault charge, but his accuser refused to testify against him. A civil claim was settled out of court. Although he protested his innocence, he later admitted that he understood why his accuser had made the allegations.

Although he preferred not to speak out on political or social issues, he felt he had to act after the murder of African-American George Floyd by a Minneapolis police officer. George was cooperating with police after they had arrested him for a minor offense, but he was hand-cuffed and restrained, with one officer holding him down with his knee on his neck. George cried out that he was choking and couldn't breathe, and people who saw what was happening begged the officer to get off him, but he did not, and George died.

Kobe and his teammates wore black shirts emblazoned with the words, "I Can't Breathe," to support the movement calling for justice for George and an awareness of the bad treatment of Black people by the police. Kobe's stand was important; *"I think it's us supporting that movement and supporting each other,"* he said.

Tragically, Kobe died in a helicopter crash in the early hours of 26 January 2020 with his thirteen-year-old daughter, Gianna, and seven others. His death caused an outpouring of grief from basketball fans.

The following year, after the Lakers won the NBA championship, they said they did it for Kobe. They chanted, "*One, two, three, Mamba!*" in the huddle before their final game, and in Los Angeles, fans cheered—remembering their idol. His Lakers teammate, LeBron James, spoke for them when he said, "*There's a lot of things that die in this world, but legends never die, and he's exactly that.*"

39

AMANDA GORMAN - POWER POET

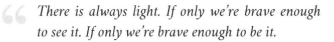 *There is always light. If only we're brave enough to see it. If only we're brave enough to be it.*

- From *The Hill We Climb* by Amanda Gorman (2021)

Many of the millions of people who watched President Joe Biden's inauguration on 20 January 2021 were captivated by the words of twenty-two-year-old poet Amanda Gorman, who recited her poem *The Hill We Climb* (written for the ceremony) with such confidence, sincerity, and poise.

Her inaugural poem called for "unity and togetherness" and implored Americans to look toward the opportunities of the future, just as a child facing adulthood, hitting the perfect note for the occasion and the start of a new era.

Amanda was born in Los Angeles on 7 March 1998. She has always loved books and writing; as a child, she had therapy for a speech impediment, and she believes this made her a better reader and writer.

Since childhood, she has cared passionately about social issues and speaking out against injustices. In 2013, she became a youth delegate for the United Nations after being inspired by Malala Yousafzai, the girl who became an international symbol of the fight for girls' education in Pakistan after she was shot for opposing the Taliban's school restrictions and awarded the Nobel Peace Prize for her stance.

In 2016, while studying sociology at Harvard University, Amanda launched One Pen One Page, a platform where young people can find programs and schemes so that *"a kid, a pen, and a page can change the world,"* and she was named National Youth Poet in 2017. That same year, she announced her intention to run for president in 2036, and she has frequently repeated this ambition in interviews since then.

She is known for being an activist as well as for her writing. She has concentrated on standing against oppression, marginalization, and racism, and she supports feminist issues and action to bring about an end to climate change. Her acclaimed 2022 poem *"Earthrise"* called for everyone to join together and save the planet.

After the shooting at the Texas elementary school in May 2022, she wrote the poem *Hymn for the Hurting*, in which she tried to express the senselessness of the tragedy and pleaded for children to be safe and for the US gun laws to be reconsidered.

Since her inauguration performance, Amanda has co-hosted the Met Gala and has been photographed for the front cover of Time Magazine and Vogue. Although she has turned down "$17 million" in endorsements that did not fit with her ethos, she became "Global Changemaker" for Estée Lauder in September 2021.

Amanda has also spoken out about her own experiences as a young Black woman, similar to those experienced every day by hundreds of thousands of people. After she had been racially profiled by a security guard near her home, she tweeted, "*This is the reality of Black girls: One day you're called an icon, the next day a threat.*" Then, after some thought—and a great deal of self-awareness—added, *"I am a Threat: a threat to injustice, to inequality, to ignorance..."*

40

COLIN KAEPERNICK - TAKING
THE KNEE

On 1 September 2016, Colin Kaepernick, the American football quarterback who had played for six seasons for the San Francisco 49ers in the National Football League (NFL) made a protest at the start of the fourth and final preseason game. During the US national anthem, he kneeled.

He said the gesture was to protest against police brutality against Black communities and issues of racial equality. He felt he could not take pride in the flag of a country that oppressed Black people.

This was not the first time he had made such a stance. Prior to his kneeling, he had sat on the bench during the anthem. Former special forces soldier Nate Bower, a fan of the 49ers, was disappointed with Colin sitting. He perceived it as a lack of patriotism and disrespect for people who had fought for their country; he had carried the coffins of comrades killed in Iraq and Afghanistan, draped with the American flag, and wrote an open letter explaining his thoughts but defending Colin's right to protest. After reading it, Colin reached out so that he could explain his perspective to him personally.

When they met, they shared a full and frank conversation and soon were far more understanding of each other's point of view. They realized that their experiences and opinions weren't so different, and Nate suggested that rather than sitting on the bench and disregarding the anthem, he might consider kneeling instead. Colin felt this was a good compromise—he had no wish to cause offense, particularly to the military.

When Colin took the knee, his teammate Eric Reid did the same, and Nate stood next to him, with his hand over his heart as the Star Spangled Banner was played.

Nate was shocked to hear the boos and jeers aimed at Colin and Eric, so loud he could hardly hear the music at times. But this gesture would be repeated—and not just in America.

Sports players and athletes from all over the world "took the knee" in solidarity with Colin, but there was a lot of criticism. Then President Donald J. Trump was appalled and pressed NFL managers and owners to fire any players who made the gesture, and in protest, more than a hundred footballers knelt the following weeks, and many spectators did the same.

It became a divisive issue in British sports. Again, players and athletes—Black and white—were often booed and subjected to racist shouts and abuse. The government refused to condemn the jeering supporters even though it had demonstrated that racism was still a major problem in sports.

Although it wasn't known to Colin when he made his protest, the British abolitionist movement in the 18th and 19th centuries had, on occasion, used the image of a kneeling enslaved man with chains on his wrists and feet, with the words, "*Am I not a Man and a Brother?*" And in 1965, Martin Luther King made that same gesture and took a knee in one of three civil rights marches in Alabama in the face of menacing armed state troopers.

As for Colin, he took a knee before every game that season and continued to speak out against police brutality, but after the season ended, no team would sign him.

Despite being widely praised and honored for his stance, he was given Sports Illustrated's Muhammad Ali Legacy Award in 2017 and Amnesty International's Ambassador of Conscience Award the following year. Although he still longs to return to his sporting career one day, if a team will sign him, in the meantime, he is one of the foremost and most influential campaigners for civil rights in America today.

CONCLUSION

The stories of Black people who have lived through and contributed to our past are incredibly diverse and far-reaching. At a time when America had its first Black president and first female Black vice president, Kamala Harris, Black history can no longer be viewed solely as stories of slavery, oppression, and abolition.

Black people have helped win wars. Josephine Baker, the American-born French singer and actress who took Paris by storm in the 1920s, worked with the Red Cross and the French Resistance in the Second World War. General Colin Powell, the first Black US Secretary of State, led America to victory during the Gulf War. In more recent years, US forces have appointed Black women to their highest levels (such as Lt. General Nadja West, the first Black US major general, and Lt. Colonel Shawna Rochelle Kimbrell, the first African American fighter pilot).

Black scientists have made their mark. In the race to halt the pandemic, Dr. Kizzmekia S. Corbett was the lead scientist on the team that developed the Moderna COVID-19 vaccine, while Dr. Ayanna Howard has taken great strides in technology—particularly artificial intelligence and robotics.

There have been Black NASA astronauts. Mae Jemison served as a mission specialist aboard the space shuttle *Endeavour* in 1992, and Victor J. Glover lived and worked on the International Space Station for an extended time.

In the world of business, there is a growing number of Black CEOs (such as David Steward, who founded World Wide Technology; Janice Bryant Howroyd, the founder of ActONE Group; and British entrepreneur and business guru Stephen Bartlett). They follow in the footsteps of Madame C.J. Walker—the first female self-made millionaire.

In culture and across all fields of the arts, there are names to be reckoned with. Dr. Shirley Thompson was the first woman in Europe to conduct and compose a symphony within forty years. Contemporary visual artist Kara Walker is known for her paintings and sculpture that explores race, gender, sexuality, violence, and identity. Misty Copeland made history as the first African-American female principal dancer with the American Ballet Theatre. In the world of cinema, directors Spike Lee, Roger Ross Williams, and Steve McQueen have made films that have challenged and delighted audiences.

Since Jesse Owens single-handedly crushed Hitler's myth of Aryan superiority on the athletics track when he won four gold medals at the 1936 Berlin Olympics, many of the world's greatest sports stars are of African heritage. Jamaican sprinter Usain Bolt is widely considered to be the greatest of all time, Simone Biles the greatest gymnast, and other Black athletes have excelled in swimming pools, ice rinks, pitches, and tracks.

There are Black campaigners who have found other issues to fight for. Dr. Robert Bullard, "the father of the environmental justice movement," and Wangari Maathai, environmentalist and founder of the Green Belt Movement, have worked tirelessly to protect our natural history and the future of the planet.

As the years progress, Black History becomes ever more rich and diverse. Studying, or being aware of history helps us to understand ourselves and the world around us and learn lessons from how we lived in the past. The experience of Black people through the ages has had a major impact on Western civilization.

Black history has come a long way, but the dream must surely be that one day, all societies, all people, and all of our pasts are so completely integrated and blended that Black history will no longer need a special month to be remembered.

Thank you for reading "What Kids Need to Know About Black History". We would love to hear from you and would be delighted if you would consider leaving us a 5-star review.

ALSO BY HILLCREST HISTORY

We plan to more release more Black History books soon, so
please follow our Author page for updates!

Made in United States
Orlando, FL
29 June 2025

62494592R00100